To Moreen,

Hope you enjoy the book.

Mebs.

27/09/23

PC Mebs
– Finding Myself

Mahmood Ahmed

authorHOUSE®

AuthorHouse™ UK
1663 Liberty Drive
Bloomington, IN 47403 USA
www.authorhouse.co.uk
Phone: UK TFN: 0800 0148641 (Toll Free inside the UK)
      UK Local: (02) 0369 56322 (+44 20 3695 6322 from outside the UK)

Published by AuthorHouse 02/22/2022

ISBN: 978-1-6655-9679-4 (sc)
ISBN: 978-1-6655-9678-7 (e)

Print information available on the last page.

About the Author

The author lives with his partner near the city of Preston, United Kingdom. He is a second generation British Asian, who came to the UK as child of 9, from Pakistan. Having worked in a variety of jobs, he finally landed his true vocation when he became a police officer with Lancashire Constabulary in 1989. After retiring in 2013, he devotes his time between mentoring young people from deprived backgrounds, working, (part-time), and running a debating society. Mahmood is passionate about learning from others and sharing perspectives on life.

Bismillah

My yesterdays shaped my todays; my todays inspire my tomorrows.

—Mahmood 'Mebs' Ahmed

To the memory of loving parents, who sadly passed away on 22 January 2013 and 4 May 2014, respectively, my mother, Siran Bi, a quiet source of compassion, dedication, and devotion, and my father, Mohammed Malik, who, uneducated and illiterate yet with the wisdom gained through the university of life, spent a lifetime being of service to others.

And to my sons, Mehboob and Bashir, and, of course, the woman who will forever be my inspiration, Marge.

Contents

Acknowledgements xiii

Introduction xv

The Early Years

Prologue 1

Chapter 1   Start of the Journey 3

Chapter 2   My Parents 21

Chapter 3   So, This Is England! 37

Chapter 4   Smoke Chimneys and Cotton Mills: Our Move
            'Up North' 49

Chapter 5   Move to the Red Rose County 75

Chapter 6   'A Prince Returning Home' 85

Chapter 7   My First Job 95

Chapter 8   My Footballing Years: The Local Asian Football
            Scene 101

Chapter 9   From Boy to Man 121

Chapter 10 'Beta, You Are Getting Married' 125

Chapter 11 On the Buses!. 129

Chapter 12 Children: A Wonderful Gift of Life. 135

Chapter 13 'Race You': A Chance Meeting That Changed
My Life!. 139

My Career with Lancashire Constabulary

Chapter 14 My Son: 'A Poleeceman'. 165

Chapter 15 Surviving the Police Training Environment. 171

Chapter 16 My Operational Years. 177

Chapter 17 A New Opportunity, a New Challenge!. 203

Chapter 18 Headhunted, Me? Pull the Other One! 223

Chapter 19 Eating 'Humble Pie' Is Not Always Bad. 227

Chapter 20 What, Me a Leader? Who Would Have Believed It!. 231

Chapter 21 The Secret Policeman Documentaries. 241

Chapter 22 The National Black Police Association 247

Chapter 23 Consolidation and Next Steps for the LBPA 259

Chapter 24 Counterterrorism 271

Chapter 25 On Reflection. 283

Acknowledgements

I was struck by Josh Lacey's acknowledgements in his book *God is Brazilian* for two reasons. Firstly, Lacey's book is on my favourite sport, football. Secondly, his encounter with an immigration official led me to think about a rather bizarre incident that inspired and pushed me into writing my book.

Even today, I find it difficult to believe what happened. But I know it's true because of the person involved. However, I'm not sure she will thank me for sharing, publicly, her unique way of encouraging me to write this book.

Just a few days before my retirement from a thoroughly enjoyable and challenging career with Lancashire Constabulary, I went to see a close colleague and a very dear friend, Ann-Marie Bull. As soon as I walked into her office, there was no small talk. Ann-Marie was like that, straight to the point with those she knew well. As I recall, she was rather excited; she quickly sat me down and just came out with it.

'Mebs, I have something to tell you. I know you are going to think it strange, very strange, but last night I … I was dreaming about you.'

Several things went through my mind. However, she instantly gave me a look that straight away told me, *No not that.* She went on, 'I dreamt that you should write a book. In fact, I got up in the middle of the night and wrote down several things you should include in your book.'

Yes, I can imagine what you are thinking. It sounded just as crazy to me. However, what a coincidence that she should have such a dream on the very night before I went to see her, only days before my retirement?

Ann-Marie sharing her dream has been a huge source of motivation for writing this book. Unfortunately, I never did get the material she wrote down; it undoubtedly would have provided much-needed excitement to my book. She had the knack of making even the mundane exciting.

Thank you, not just for inspiring me to write this book, Ann-Marie, but also for being a very dear friend, if somewhat a little (or perhaps a lot) weird.

I also want to thank my publishers, Author House; Sarah Cantelo for the editorial support; Raj Patel for designing the book covers; and all my former colleagues, my friends, and my family for their support.

Finally, I want to thank the woman who has stuck by me through thick and thin, for all her inspiration and support. Marge, it took your love to awaken me from my daydreaming. Thank you from the bottom of my heart.

Introduction

This book is my attempt to put forward a very ordinary but, on reflection, quite fulfilling journey—a journey that took a young boy from a rural village in Pakistan to a whole new and unexpected life in multicultural England. It is as passionate, honest, critical, and constructive as my limited ability allows. While an autobiography is, selfishly, all about the author, I very much hope it doesn't come across as totally selfish and that it's of interest to anyone who reads it.

The book is split into two parts—my early years and my years with Lancashire Constabulary. In the first part, I focus on my early years in Pakistan, sharing memories of my childhood, my extended family, our way of life, the games we children played, and my time at school. I also share my father's journey to the 'other side of the world' and how my mother and I came to join him three years later.

I capture my transition from a teenager to a young man, my personality, my early experiences of life in this country—including discrimination—some of my key influencers, and how I became hooked on 'the beautiful game'. My schooling years in this country are included, as is my marriage, the birth of my two sons, and a chance meeting that changed my life. It covers the period from 1965 to 1989.

The second part focuses on my career as a police officer with Lancashire Constabulary and my journey towards middle age, covering the period between 1989 and 2013. It deals with me coming to terms with who I was and who I had become—showing how, once a shy daydreamer, I become someone with the ability to support, guide, and influence others.

This is a journey of an incredibly introverted and timid boy who eventually finds himself through the devotion and love of a wonderfully patient woman and through the teachings of many people, enabling him to fulfil his father's dream of 'being a service to others'.

Part I

The Early Years

Prologue

The beginning of the end

It is the middle of September 2013. I am in the sports and social club at Lancashire Constabulary's headquarters. My sons, Mehboob and Bashir, are with me, as is the woman who has been with me ever since we met. The large room at the bar is filled with my colleagues and decorated by my dear friend Lukmaan Mulla with photos of many of my police memories. The gathering is to mark my retirement as a police officer and as the chair of the Lancashire Black Police Association (LBPA). I am honoured and privileged to have so many people at my leaving do, including the whole chief officer team—something rarely afforded to a mere PC.

I was the chair of the LBPA for over ten years—as far as I am aware, the longest tenure for such a post in the country. As I share my pride and joy with my family and friends, I also reflect on a journey that started thousands of miles away. I am finding it hard to believe the transformation that has taken place. I have gone from a shy and unassuming little boy who was always daydreaming to a man who dedicated himself to making a difference for others.

I have not only 'survived' a career within the police service—embedded with challenges, danger, and discrimination—I have also found it rewarding and satisfying, going on to influence at the highest level within the police service.

Please allow me to start my story at the beginning.

Chapter 1

Start of the Journey

My journey began in the 1950s, the so-called rock and roll years.

I am led to believe I was born in 'about 1956'. I say *about*, as that is precisely what it says on my birth certificate. Whatever the exact year, it was an extremely special year for one ordinary couple in an unremarkable village in Pakistan. For my parents, my birth provided a new hope—that of their fifth born surviving beyond his first birthday.

Fight for survival

My birthplace, Kala Gujran, lies approximately two hours' drive from the Pakistani capital, Islamabad, and approximately ten minutes' drive from the city of Jhelum. Kala Gujran has seen a huge population growth but has had limited progress and development as far as quality of life is concerned. It is a village, like many others, crippled with corruption and poverty. Agriculture is the mainstay of its inhabitants. Electricity reached the village between me leaving in 1965 and my first visit back in 1975. However, it is turned on and off as and when it suits the authorities. Without electricity, it's unbearably hot during the summer months, with temperatures reaching over fifty degrees Celsius, and extremely cold in the winter months.

Some of the population growth in the village has been due to the relocation of people from the 'old Dadyal' in Mirpur after it was flooded and, more recently, that of migrants from neighbouring Afghanistan. The landscape around my village, compared to the lush green fields of England, is dry and dusty. Open sewers run down the middle or along the sides of every street, attracting flies, rats, and disease.

Living there, I never noticed any of this. What was constantly around me as I grew up became my norm, and I only noticed these differences after moving to my new environment in England.

When I first returned to my village, the scene that greeted me was hard to comprehend. *How could this be?* I asked myself. *How can there be so many incredibly poor people in the village? How can God allow this?* I struggle, even today, to answer those questions, although now I no longer blame God or religion.

I am aware that, despite the poverty, Pakistan has a good tourist trade, with some places of outstanding beauty, which, as a child, I never got to see. Irrespective of the issues and challenges Kala Gujran faces, it is the place of my birth and my roots, and it will always hold a special place in my heart.

No one knows exactly when I was born. Keeping official records, such as birth or marriage certificates, was not common practice in Pakistan at the time. Working on the land, tending to the animals, and producing enough food for the family were everyone's main priorities. There was little or no need for such documents. Travelling outside the village was a rarity; travelling outside the country was practically unheard of. However, this started to change by the late 1950s and early 1960s. Stories about people travelling abroad, especially to England, began to circulate from village to village.

England was a country still rebuilding following the Second World War. In England you could earn enough money not only to support your family but also to help others within your village. Many families and other villagers pooled their resources to send someone to this land of plenty. That's how my father came to be chosen as one of the village 'pioneers'. In 1962, he left his family for this faraway country, hoping to return home as quickly as possible, having accumulated enough funds to meet the needs of the family and the village.

Three years later, he realised it was not to be. Naturally, my father, like others, longed to be with his family again. He wanted us to join him in England—hence, the need for documentation.

To join my father, we had to have a passport for my mother and a birth certificate for me made. My mother's passport also included my photograph and my father's details. Both documents were hurriedly obtained from Jhelum, where all the clerical administration was carried out for nearby villages.

I still have a copy of my birth certificate, which states that I was born in Kala Gujran, in *about* 1956. No day or month is given, presumably because no one from my family could remember those details. I have no idea as to why 11 November was chosen as the day and month of my birth. I am also led to believe that I am approximately two years older than stated on my birth certificate and my passport. My parents reduced my age, as I looked much younger than my years, and they were worried in case the immigration officials at Heathrow airport disputed my age and rejected my entry into the country.

Please don't tell the Border Agency. What with the Windrush scandal, you never know what they might do to me. I promise this is a recent discovery, and I knew nothing about it at the time!

***

One of my most vivid childhood memories is of being plagued with childhood illnesses. Fever rarely left my body. I had constant stomach pains and ongoing problems with my eyes. I was far from a healthy child.

My illnesses were not due to malnutrition. Lack of hygiene or sanitation perhaps played a role, but certainly not lack of food. I don't ever remember going hungry. I do, though, recall not wearing shoes, just like all the other children. In the summer when the ground was baking hot, we had to jump from one small patch of grass onto another to avoid getting our feet burned.

Living conditions were similar for most in the village, all living off the land apart from a few rich landowning families.

Why was I so ill? What were the causes? The question is not easy to answer after all these years, especially with those who may have been able to help now long gone. I have been told I was always a sickly child. However, having survived past my first birthday, I had already outlived all my siblings. Unfortunately, no one has been able to tell me how my siblings died, except to say that, at the time, young children's survival rates were very low.

I am aware of the phrase 'third time lucky'. In my case, it was definitely 'fifth time lucky'. The fifth born, I was the only one of my parents' children to survive beyond infancy, gradually getting stronger.

After my sixth birthday, I developed severe stomach pains. These were a direct result of the treatment I'd received at the hands of a so-called doctor. I had fallen off the family donkey and was taken to see someone who treated everyone with any kind of illness or injury if they could afford to pay. He was referred to as a doctor, though he was probably not qualified. He gave me several injections, as he could not find what was wrong with me and probably felt that, to get paid, he had to give me something as medication.

Children falling from donkeys is normal in Pakistan. Usually, these incidents are quite hilarious, resulting in injury only to one's ego and pride. However, in my case, it was a little more serious. I was with my cousin George about whom you will read more later and who was only two years younger than me. We were riding our donkey back to our farm from our house in the village. We'd only gone a few hundred yards when a group of boys thought it would be hilarious to see what the 'beast of burden' would do if they belted it with a stick.

The poor thing squealed in pain and shot off like a wild bull. We managed to hang on for a few yards but were then flung off. George felt some pain in his left arm but thought nothing of it. I, however, escaped without injury—or so it seemed. We both went chasing after the terrified animal and managed to catch up with it, grazing on a patch of grass nearby. We decided to walk the poor animal the rest of the way to the farm.

When we got to the farm, we were met by one of our male relatives. I didn't know it then, but he was to become my future father-in-law. He didn't seem interested in what had happened to us and told us to go back home.

We did not argue and set off walking home. We'd only gone a few hundred yards when, suddenly, everything started to go dark for me.

Very quickly, I began to lose my sight. I was terrified. Not knowing what was happening, I panicked.

At first, George thought I was messing about and did not believe me, but I started to scream and yell at him, 'I can't see! I can't see.' This, in turn, frightened him. He told me to sit down beside the dirt road, whilst he went back to the farm to get help.

He came back within a few minutes. Apparently, my future father-in-law didn't believe him and told George to stop messing about and go home.

I don't remember much after that or how I got home. But I do remember waking up in bed sometime later and asking for my mother. More worryingly, I didn't recognise anyone around me. I was becoming delirious and started swearing and shouting at anyone who came near me. I kept asking for my mother, before being soothed back to sleep by my grandmother. Each time I woke up, I would start screaming and shouting, still not able to see.

Unfortunately, my mother had gone on a pilgrimage to one of the holy shrines, something the women did on a regular basis.

My erratic and unusual behaviour upset my grandmother. She immediately dispatched the youngest of my father's two brothers, Ali Ahmed, to fetch my mother and not to return without her.

When my mother arrived, upon seeing me in bed surrounded by several people, her heart sank, almost collapsing to the floor. Later she told me her mind had gone back to the terrible time when 'God' took away all her other children, and she thought she was going to lose me too.

Apparently, when I fell from the donkey, I banged my head on a stone and had what you might call a delayed reaction. I suffered temporary blindness, concussion, and short-term memory loss, which lasted for several days. During those few days, I also fell in and out of consciousness. Everyone in the family became seriously worried, but no one wanted to tell my father, who was in England. They were scared he would blame them and return home immediately.

Luckily, within days, I began to get both my sight and my memory back and made a full recovery. My mother and all my extended family believe I only survived due to the prayers of many of the villagers. Lots of them prayed for me due to the respect and high esteem they held for my father.

As I started to get better, my mother decided to take me to see some of the more renowned holy men, or 'pirs' as they are known, and their shrines. The pirs were paid to pray for my health and to keep me safe.

Many Muslims, all over the world, visit their pirs and their holy shrines as part of their religious beliefs. Often pirs are invited to visit their *shagirds* (students or devotees) in countries all over the world, including Britain, for blessings, consultations, and prayers to help ease their life, their pains, and other ills or to simply thank the pirs. Shagirds usually pay all expenses and upkeep of their pirs, while showering them with gifts. Other shagirds who visit make further payments upon seeking advice, guidance, or spiritual healing.

My mother and my family believe that the prayers of the pirs and those of the villagers saved my life. I may not be as religious as my parents, but I do believe the prayers of sincere people are always answered, perhaps not always in ways that are obvious to us.

The other thing that really stands out with regards to my health is the annual problems with my eyes. If anyone suffered with this kind of ailment, as I recall it was always the children, they were taken to an elderly 'enlightened' woman in the village.

Mahmood Ahmed

At a certain time of the year, usually summertime, my eyes would become very swollen and painful. There would be a build-up of thick, yellowy discharge around my eyelids, making them sore to touch, sensitive to light, and difficult to open. This lasted for up to two weeks. I vividly remember, in pain, being taken to see this old lady. She would wash my eyes, but she was not at all gentle; in fact, she was very rough. I recall screaming my head off at the very thought of having to visit her. She would also put some black powdery substance called *Surma* in my eyes; it burned and stung my eyes. The pain only eased when I eventually fell asleep.

Surma is something many Asians, particularly Pakistanis, still use, even in the United Kingdom, believing it to clean their eyes.

All in all, it was not the best start to my life. However, unlike so many other children and my own siblings, I survived.

Other memories of my village and childhood

Although I have lived in England for more than fifty years, time has not deprived me of many of my memories of the place I was born in. Some of those memories of my childhood, my extended family, and the village remain in my mind, available to recall whenever I want to. Some were rekindled by my visits back there; others have never faded. I am pleased to say that these are, overall, happy memories. I hope some will, as I share them, bring a smile to your face, while others may leave you a little sad or puzzled.

There is so much I could tell you about my village that I never knew as a child. For instance, the region is where Alexander the Great fought battles to persuade his soldiers to continue their march further into India. The Gujjars, from which the village derives its name, were known as the 'martyrs and warriors', and it was in this region where the Battle of Chillianwala took place, where the British were defeated in the Second Anglo-Sikh War.

Following partition in 1947, there was war and conflict between India and Pakistan, with immense suffering and death on both sides. I remember as children having the fear of God instilled in us about the Indian planes coming to bomb Pakistan. It remained like that during the wars between the two countries for several decades. Unfortunately, the threat of war remains today, with tensions between the two countries over Kashmir flaring up from time to time.

I personally do not recall our village ever being bombed by the Indian planes, but I do remember hearing the terrifying sound of the planes. Then there were the stories told by village elders about these planes chasing people down, shooting and killing them as they ran for cover. Any sound of such planes used to terrify us children, and we would run inside shouting and screaming.

Having moved to England and my new comfortable surroundings, I learnt the important part surroundings and environment play in forming our perceptions of others—in my case, of the Indian people.

In recent years, when I have read and watched documentaries about India's divide, I've learned more about the terrible atrocities committed on both sides—hundreds of thousands of innocent women, children, and men butchered by Muslims, Hindus, and Sikhs alike.

Yet it was not always like that. My mother has spoken of times, before the separation, when Sikhs and Muslims lived peacefully side by side. She has mentioned the closeness between the Sikhs and the Muslims that even the cutting up of India could not destroy. This was still evident when we came to England, and my father formed a lifelong friendship with a Sikh man and his family while they worked together in Oxford.

***

Baby goat

The next memory relates to what we would call a family pet in this country. Due to the circumstances and the way we lived our life in Pakistan, I am not sure that any animal owned by families there could ever be regarded as pets. Most animals were working animals, whether to help farm the land, act as beasts of burden, guard property, or provide food. All animals had their roles. Cats were chief ratcatchers; dogs served as guards; cows, hens, goats, sheep, and so on were all sources of food and potential income; oxen worked the land; and donkeys were a form of transport.

I would have been about five or six years old when I was given a baby goat to look after. I was so proud to be given this responsibility; none of my cousins had such responsibility. The baby goat was light brown in colour, with clear white patches around the mouth, eyes, and ears. I fell in love with it straight away, and within days, everywhere I went, the kid was sure to follow. The time I spent with this baby goat was my happiest of all in Pakistan. I would feed it, play with it, and take it for walks around the farm, not allowing anyone else near it. It would chase me, knock me down, and jump in the air with me. I'd cuddle it as if it was my little brother or sister. I had so much affection for it.

For the next few months, I even stopped playing with my friends so I could spend as much time as possible with my goat. Strange as it may sound, it had no name, since animals in Pakistan were not given names. I guess it's probably because they're not considered pets in the first place, so a name was unnecessary.

Unfortunately, my goat grew up too quickly, and it had to be either sold to help towards the family upkeep or sacrificed as part of a religious ceremony. My little goat was sacrificed. I was heartbroken and cried my eyes out for days, even though my grandmother explained why it had to be sacrificed. I was too young to understand. It took months for me to get over the loss of my poor little goat. I vowed never to allow myself to get close to another animal ever again. It had quite a profound effect on me and my future inability to get close to animals. I stopped going to our farm for a long time afterwards.

This fuelled my shy personality, which was developing more rapidly than I realised, sowing the early seeds that would make it difficult for me to talk to people or make friends.

Schooldays

I was fortunate enough to be able to go to school. It was a luxury not afforded to many children in the village. The fact that I could go to school was simply down to my father being in England. He was able not only to send enough money to make things easier for my grandmother, the head of the family, but also to support my schooling, which he insisted on.

When my father first came to England, everyone expected him to work for a few years, earn enough money, and return home—well, everyone except me, that is. I was certain I would join him in England. I was convinced that was the only reason my father wanted me to go to school.

At school we had no pens or books to write in. We used small wooden boards called *Tukhtees* to write on. These were about a foot long, six inches wide, and about half an inch thick. They had a handle carved out at one end so they could easily be carried. Each day, after use they needed to be washed and plastered with a thin layer of mud and dried before being reused. For pens, we used a small, thin wooden stick about six inches long, sharpened and shaped at one end into a writing tip like a quill, before being dipped into ink.

In class, on many occasions I'd be caught drawing what appeared to be squiggly lines at the top of my Tukhtee. One day, my teacher finally asked me what these lines were. I calmly replied, 'These are not lines, sir. This is English. I am writing in English.'

He said nothing. Instead, he had a bemused look on his face that said it all. He must have thought. *This poor boy is away with the fairies!*

I didn't let that bother me. In my mind, I was preparing for my life in England.

***

Another happy memory I have as a boy is dancing in the rain outside my house in the street with other children. Rain was God sent for the farmers; it provided much-needed water for their crops. However, for the children, it was an opportunity to play and dance when the heavens opened. And boy did they open. When it rained in Pakistan, it very quickly turned into torrential downpour. But the feeling of large droplets of water falling on your face and onto your tongue as you opened your mouth to taste them was exhilarating—something I have never been able to feel in this country, despite all the rain we have here!

I guess it was something that could only happen at a carefree phase that comes along once in a lifetime. I will never forget that simple pleasure.

Childhood games

I don't remember lots of games we played as children, but the two that are etched most strongly in my mind are marbles and gilli-danda .

The way we played marbles in Pakistan is vastly different to the way they are played in England. We did not simply roll our marbles; we used our middle or index finger to catapult or shoot them at the other marbles, requiring much more skill than simply rolling them.

Gilli-danda was by far the favourite game of all among the children in our village, and certainly the one I loved the best. It was played by two or more players using two wooden sticks. One stick was about two feet long and roughly an inch or so in diameter. The other stick was much smaller—six to eight inches long, the same width, and sharpened at both ends. You dig a small, narrow channel—about six inches long, two inches deep, and two inches wide—into the ground like a groove.

The 'batsman' placed the small stick across the groove and, with the larger stick, flicked it as far as possible, keeping it as low as possible to avoid it being caught by the fielders. The fielders tried to catch it; if they failed, they would then throw it at the large stick, which would be placed flat on the ground over the groove.

If the small stick hit the larger stick, the batsman would be out. If not, the batsman would use the larger stick to flick one of the sharpened ends of the small stick and, whilst it was still in the air, hit it as hard as possible, trying not to get caught. The fielders would again try to catch it, and if they failed, they would again try and hit the larger stick. This process was repeated until the batsmen were all out. The fielding side then got to bat. There were no runs involved that I recall, so I'm not sure how winning was decided.

In all my visits back (the first one was after ten years), I never saw either of these games being played by any of the children. More modern games like cricket had come to the village.

As I write about these two games, another one comes to mind— quite a violent game called *muckka*. At the time, it seemed to be all the rage. But looking back on it now, it seems a very strange and dangerous game for young boys to play (all these games were played by boys only, since our culture forbids the mixing of boys and girls).

Muckka is a Punjabi word for 'fist'. This game can be played by two or more players, but it was usually played by just two players. The rules were simple. Once both players had agreed to play, if they were in sight of each other, they had to have one of their arms folded behind their back with a clenched fist. If a player was spotted by the opponent without his arm in exactly this position, then his opponent could punch him in the back as hard as he could. You automatically lost the game if you hit your opponent anywhere else. Quite often, players would sneak up on each other, trying to catch each other out.

I remember doubling up in pain many times, having been caught out. It brings back painful memories. The game would only end when both players agreed to call it quits; sometimes this would take days, and often you forgot you were still playing the game and paid for it painfully.

Finally, how could I forget good old hide-and-seek, a game we all enjoyed and one that is universally known and loved. Rural villages like ours were ideal for this game, with so many dark alleys and unlit streets and houses. The bright moonlight in Pakistan was amazing, something else I have never witnessed in this country to the same extent. Although the darkness was rather scary, being frightened, in a weird way, added to the attraction of the game.

There was no such thing as antisocial behaviour or adults frightening you about 'stranger danger'. It was such a carefree time; as children, we had never heard of the word 'crime'. If something awful took place, it took place somewhere else, another village, another region—not in our village.

Other happy memories include the annual fairs that came to the village and the fasting period during the month of Ramadan, followed by the Eid celebrations. Eid marked the end of a period of around thirty days of fasting, depending on the sighting of the moon. When fasting, you are not allowed any water or food from sunrise to sunset. This is much harder during the summer months, as the days are longer, and fasting can be for up to eighteen hours a day. All Muslim adults must fast, as well as healthy children from ten upwards. It was at Eid that I remember all the extended family coming together, with invitations to each other's homes for food and merriment. Once a year, everyone got to wear their new clothes. It was also at these celebrations that we enjoyed food only cooked at Eid, such as lamb, beef, or chicken curries; samosas, pakoras, and kebabs; sweet multicoloured rice with sultanas, almonds, and coconut; and semolina, again with sultanas and almond or coconut. The food would last for days, but the highlight for us children was when an adult put up a swing for us on the giant oak tree that we had in our huge courtyard. We absolutely loved this annual treat, as there were no playgrounds with swings, seesaws, and roundabouts, as in this country.

Mahmood Ahmed

Kala Gujran village

Kala Gujran has what can loosely be called two main roads. Both were very muddy and uneven, with the odd patch of tarmac dotted here and there and many potholes. The last time I visited, in 2014, there were some attempts being made to tarmac one of them—the one that runs from the main GT (Grand Trunk) Road through the village towards Chak Jamal, right outside our house. The roadworks, I was told, had been going on for nearly three years. Whilst there, I never saw anyone doing any work.

In the bazaar, there was the usual hustle and bustle associated with such a place. People ate or drank tea and always talked—often, as is the Pakistani way, loudly. People bartered or haggled over prices, not the sort of thing the reserved British would do; others rushed to get to wherever they need to be.

The shops in the bazaar sold everything you could want—clothes, shoes, books, hardware, and various foods and spices. And if you didn't see what you wanted, the shopkeepers would promise to either get it for you or make it for you. In this sense, they were very inventive. The shopkeepers' children ran errands for them or just ran around shouting to attract business. The bazaar also had many animals, which either belonged to the shopkeepers or were being used to transport goods, often causing chaos. There were cyclists and people on horse carriages (*tangays*), all adding to the unique atmosphere of the bazaar.

As children, we never had any money to buy sweets. My only treat was when my uncle Ghani, on my mother's side, visited on leave from the army. He would always bring a bag of sweets and a small amount of sugar—a treat for all the family.

We may not have been able to buy sweets as children, but we did pick wild berries and fruits, particularly mangoes from trees that grew wild. Some children picked fruit from trees in people's gardens—the naughty ones among us, that is. I never had the courage to do that, being a goody two shoes.

Tangays were stationed at both ends of the bazaar, ready to transport people to Jhelum city or other nearby villages. From Jhelum, people could catch a bus or a train to places further afield, although you could always hail down a bus anywhere along GT Road. There were never any problems with a bus being full, since people were herded on irrespective of numbers.

As a small boy, I never saw any cars in the village. Occasionally, a group of us would go and sit by the side of GT Road, hours on end, waiting to see one zoom past. A train going by was an even bigger and rarer treat.

It was a sign of the times that many of the children and quite a lot of the adults wore no shoes. Those who had a pair were the lucky ones. I must have had a pair, as I remember wearing them when visiting my mum's relatives in Dadyal. They must have been my only pair, used for special occasions.

It never occurred to me to think about the clothes I wore or the condition they were in, until I saw what people were wearing here in England. In my village, people wore whatever they could afford, usually the same salwar kameez (long shirt and trousers), perhaps with a thick jumper in the winter. The men and women would also wear a thick woollen sheet or 'chador in the winter. The women always had their heads covered by a dupatta, or scarf, while the men wore turbans or hats. However, everyone wore their best or cleanest clothes for Friday prayers, much like people wearing their Sunday best when going to church here.

All the children and adults had greasy hair, due to using mustard oil, which somehow everyone was able to afford. I must admit, I didn't like it, but none of us suffered from itchy scalp or dandruff.

As mentioned previously, I used to visit Dadyal with my mother during the holidays. Dadyal is approximately three hours' drive from Kala Gujran, travelling north. It is mountainous and much more scenic than Kala Gujran, which added to my excitement on visits to my relatives there.

The extended family there seemed to be much bigger for some reason, with lots of children my age. I saw life in Kala Gujran as rather hard work; Dadyal, in comparison, seemed more fun. Time there was spent swimming in the tarns, playing marbles or gooli danda with my cousins and their friends. My visits there were cut short far too quickly, as the holidays ended, and we went back to Kala Gujran.

Chapter 2

My Parents

I am ashamed to say, when I was growing up, I had little thoughts for anyone or anything other than myself, including my parents. Thinking about how life may have been for them only began when I became an adult.

However, as a schoolboy in England, I was sometimes asked by some of the other children what life was like in Pakistan. In those days, there was little in our books about how people in other parts of the world lived. In Oxford, on rare occasions, our teacher would ask me to share something about where I came from and say a few words about my parents, prompting questions from the other children.

Looking back, I can now see how some children may have grown up knowing little about other cultures, customs, and faiths and how some may have formed negative perceptions about those different to them.

Similar questions were once again asked of me when I became a police officer, many years later. Just as it was at school, on my initial police training course, I was asked to talk about my culture and what it was like for my parents when they came to this country. The trainers used this 'talk', as part of their diversity training. It's fair to say that my colleagues showed genuine interest, although I found the questions difficult to deal with due to my lack of confidence in talking to groups of people and being shy and nervous.

Some of the questions my classmates and colleagues asked were quite similar. What did your parents do in Pakistan? Why did they want to come to England? The children also wanted to know what our house was like. Did I have a pet? What team did I support? In addition, my colleagues wanted to know about my religion and culture: Why do Muslims fast? Do all Muslims have to go to Mecca? Will all Muslims go to heaven? Why do some Muslim women cover their faces? How did your parents meet? Was it an arranged marriage?

Despite being incredibly nervous, I was able to answer most of these, although I struggled with some questions about my parents and was quite embarrassed by how little I knew about them.

Looking back on my childhood in Pakistan, it seems my early life was spent with my mother and grandmother; in fact, most of it was spent with my grandmother, as was the norm for many children, with parents working the land or working on the land for others.

My father

Quality time with fathers was never heard of; this seems to be very much a Western thing, even today. Fathers in the Pakistani culture are regarded as central figures of authority and respect. They are the source of the family's income and reputation; they form the basis of the family's identity and standing within the community. Mothers and women generally earn respect by being silent and invisible. Yet, as in many cultures, they are the backbone of all family life.

In our culture, in my humble opinion, children's respect for their parents and elders is usually out of fear, drilled into them from an early age, whilst questioning elders is certainly not allowed. Also, you never look elders in the eye; lowering your gaze is a sign of respect. The combination of my culture and my own shy personality made looking everyone in the eye difficult for me. Even today, I remind myself to maintain eye contact when talking to people.

I do not recall having many father-and-son moments. And judging from my experiences of my extended family, this is still very much the norm for many second- and third-generation Pakistanis. Mothers are the ones who show any tender moments, just like mothers all over the world. They are also the ones who discipline you.

From my memories of my father and from what little I have been told by those around me, I know he spent a lot of time away from home. Like his brothers, he worked long hours on the farm. But he also worked for the army as a barber, which took him away from the family.

My grandmother often told me about his army days; she would say that my father was very well liked by the soldiers, despite being a barber—a profession and caste that is looked down on in our culture. However, he was popular because he was a renowned kabaddi player, representing his unit across the region.

I remember one story she told me. I guess it reflected my father's response to anyone who showed little respect for others, especially those who were condescending towards those deemed to be of a lower caste or standing in society.

One day, he was cutting a senior officer's hair when the officer spoke to him in an abrupt and condescending manner, telling him how privileged he was to be cutting his hair. My father just flipped. Picking up the chair with the officer in it, he flung it outside onto the drill square and stormed off to his room, preparing to leave immediately. Many of the soldiers, including other senior officers, tried to persuade him to stay, even promised to get him an apology. But he wouldn't hear of it; he told them that nobody had the right to speak to another man like that, no matter what their rank. He wouldn't put up with it from anyone. He simply walked out and got himself a job with another army unit.

As a highly respected kabaddi player, my father travelled frequently to take part in tournaments across the Jhelum region, representing his unit or his village. At that time, kabaddi was a national sport in Pakistan, nearly as popular as cricket and hockey—in some regions, more so than both. It's played by two opposing teams, with an agreed number of players, usually around seven on each side. The rules are straightforward; the playing surface or 'pitch' is split into two halves, as in football, but a little smaller. Each player takes it in turn to tag one of the players in the opposing half and then try to make it back to his own half of the pitch. Only the player he tags on the opposing team can prevent him from returning to his own half, using whatever means at his disposal. This is where the strength, agility, and speed of players is tested. Whichever team has the most players who make it back, once every player has had a go, wins.

Unlike cricket and hockey, kabaddi players are not paid by the team they represent; rather, spectators lavish players with cash during and after the game. With his strength, power, and athleticism, my father made more money from one kabaddi game than he did working for months on the farm. His involvement in kabaddi helped supplement the family's income. It also helped to enhance his reputation throughout the Jhelum district.

Several of my family members have told me about my father's physical strength and power, speaking proudly about it. My grandmother would talk about how immensely strong and powerful he was, quickly adding that he also had a temper on him. I'm sure that all these stories about his strength and power and quick temper helped create a heroic image of him, but also one of fear.

My physical build, both as a boy and as a man, is nothing to shout about. Compared with my father, I am thin and gangly, weak, and sickly. From what I've been told about my father, I assumed he only respected those with similar attributes to himself. This was a disservice in my early assumptions to a proud and private man who loved his family.

However, my father's courage and strength have served the family well. I remember another story I was told by my grandmother about how he dealt with a gang of thieves who tried to steal our crops.

A notorious gang was operating in several villages, including ours. They would steal machinery, animals, and crops, particularly from small farms like ours. Reporting the theft to the police was a complete waste of time, as a 'fee' had to be paid, which many could not afford.

There had been several reports of farms having fallen victim to mainly crop theft, with the gang striking in the early hours of the morning. My father wasn't going to become another victim without a fight. In anticipation, he would hide within the crop fields, armed with a long pole, like those carried by Robin Hood and his merry men, waiting for the thieves. The thought of my father as the Robin Hood of the village added to the excitement of the story.

Nothing happened for several nights, and then one night, he heard voices and the sound of crops being cut. He crept silently towards the field where the noise was coming from and saw a group of four men chopping away at the crops.

He leapt out, swinging his pole, startling the men, and catching one of them between the shoulder blades. The surprised men dropped their tools and ran off. He expected them to come back with reinforcements, but the gang never returned. My grandmother said they, too, had heard about his reputation but didn't realise they were on his farm.

In my eyes, my father's legend grew and grew, but unfortunately, so did my fear of him. I was unable to differentiate between the two.

Though my father had never laid a hand on me, the more stories I was told about his physical prowess, the more fearful I became. I do not know why his strength, courage, and desire to stand up for others, to protect and fight for them, would frighten me so much. It should have brought me closer to him, as sporting achievement and helping others are qualities I admire greatly.

Growing up in England, seeing white fathers playing in the park with their children, I so much wanted my father to do the same with me. Understanding norms in diverse cultures, including my own, was something I only began to grasp much later in my life and realised it wasn't the norm for Pakistani fathers. Despite my fear of my father, strangely, I have always felt he loved me deeply. I felt a sense of security that only he could provide. I learned to put down the lack of open affection as a cultural norm. Perhaps this might be difficult for some to understand in Western society, but I am sure you have all heard about unspoken feelings or unspoken love. I felt this from my father—in fact, from both my parents, even though they never actually told me.

Regrettably, fearing the father is a pattern that has inadvertently been repeated by both my sons too. Mehboob and Bashir, in recent conversations, have told me that they had been 'terrified' of me throughout their childhood and their early adulthood. I was shocked when I first heard it. They said it was not because I hit them or even shouted at them. After I left the family home, their grandmother and mother used to frighten them with stories of what I would do if they misbehaved. I noticed how reluctant they were to approach me when I went to visit them. It took them a while to relax, and they only did so when we were away from their family home.

I've mentioned that my father was a hard-working fearless individual, with strong morals and ethics. It was all these qualities that helped the village elders decide who best to send to England. By the early 1960s, rumours had reached the village about people from nearby villages travelling to 'Inglaand', making much money for their families and their village.

Our village elders decided to do the same. I am told it was touch-and-go whether our village could pool enough money together to be able to pay for his fare and a small amount for his keep. They asked everyone to contribute, in whatever way they could. Some sold a chicken, a cow, even crops to help my father get to England.

I don't know how my father felt about travelling thousands of miles to work in a country whose language he did not speak. What I do know is that my father was the kind of person who would do anything to help, when asked. When told that, by accepting this opportunity, he would be helping the whole village, he jumped at it.

In fact, one of the few things he did say to me as a child was, 'Your life is meaningless unless it is of service to others.'

I have never forgotten his words, endeavouring to do that all my life—even as a child, in Pakistan. Then the only way I could help others was to give money to the poor, which I did when my father sent some for me. I felt the need of the poor was much greater than mine.

I was also encouraged to give to the poor by my mother; she used to tell me it would help me to get to heaven. Giving to charities, not just financially, has become an important part of my adult life and, I am proud to say, part of my sons' lives too.

Years later I read a short piece, by Emily Dickinson:

> If I can stop one heart from breaking,
> I shall not live in vain.
> If I can ease one life the aching,
> Or cool one pain,
> Or help one fainting robin
> Unto his nest again,
> I shall not live in vain.

This helped me put into perspective what my father meant by a life of service to others. He wanted to be there for all who he could help. The term 'server' originally meant someone who assisted a priest. I believe my father's lifetime of devotion to others' service was because of his strong religious beliefs.

What my parents taught me, along with that short piece by Dickinson, has helped focus my efforts—in both my professional and my personal life—to try and do what I can for others.

My father never forgot what some of the villagers did for him, when they sacrificed what they could. When he first started working in England, he sent 50 per cent of his wage to the village elders and 30 per cent to his family and kept the remainder for his upkeep. By the time he retired, he was still sending 20 per cent of his wage to the elders for them to support the village, even though he had repaid his debt many times over.

Despite the precious little quality time my father and I spent together, during the few conversations we had, he did tell me the following story when he first arrived in England. It also changed my long-held view of Pakistani men and their lack of sense of humour.

The story took place when my mother and I had just arrived to join my father in England. We had visitors, which was what tended to happen whenever new arrivals came. In those days, apart from writing to each other, the only other form of communication between families was messages brought by the new arrivals, who also came bearing gifts and items of food.

My father began by telling everyone that he came on a PIA (Pakistan International Airlines) flight from Karachi to Heathrow, full of young Pakistani men hoping to make lots of money in this wonderful country. He said he didn't know anyone on the plane, and there was no one going to Oxford. Once they had all made their way through customs, some were met by those they knew, while others began to make their way towards buses and trains. Those who could speak a few words of English helped others to get on the right buses and trains, whilst some shared taxis to their destinations. My father was helped onto a bus bound for Oxford.

By the time he arrived in Oxford, it was early evening and already dark. All he had was a piece of paper with an address and a small tattered old suitcase with a few of his belongings. He had no way of knowing how he was to make his way to the address in Oxford. When he got off the bus, instead of asking someone for directions at the bus station, he set off walking. He soon found himself wandering around the deserted town centre. He continued walking aimlessly, hoping to bump into someone who may be able to point him in the right direction.

He eventually spotted a group of people inside a shop. He walked up to them, but as he did not speak any English, he pointed to the piece of paper and waited for a response. A moment later, he again pointed to the piece of paper. Still no response. For the third time, he pointed to the piece of paper in his hand, this time more forcefully. Again, no response. Feeling rather dejected, and with his perceptions of kindness of the locals shattered, he walked off. Luckily, after walking round in circles for some time, he came across a man who could see that he was lost and didn't speak any English, so he took him to his address. His faith in the kindness of the locals was once again restored.

As he continued with the story, he told us that the landlord, called Raja Bostan, also acted as interpreter for all new arrivals, took them shopping, and helped them find jobs. The day after my father's arrival, he was taken shopping by Raja. My father desperately needed clothes, as the ones he had brought with him were woefully inadequate for the British winter. They were in the city centre, and as they went past the shop where my father had seen the group of people the previous night, he stopped and started to smile. Raja looked at him, rather taken aback by my father's strange behaviour. He asked him why he was smiling. My father pointed at the group inside the window and said, 'I was getting really angry with them last night, as they wouldn't speak to me.' He was pointing to a group of mannequins. They both broke out in laughter.

My father had never seen mannequins before, and when he'd seen them the previous night, in the dark, he'd mistaken them for real people. But it was the fact that he was able to share this with us, in front of all his friends, laughing at himself, that provided me with a different perspective of him and some of the other Pakistani men.

They do have a sense of humour after all! I thought.

Although my father had a reputation for being brave and fearless, in an unexpected and rare father-and-son moment, he admitted to being terrified of coming to this country. What if he failed to settle? What if he couldn't get a job? And what if he didn't earn enough money to support his family or pay back all those who had placed such huge faith in him? It is only now that I realise how heavy a burden it must have been for him and others like him who came to this country for the 'collective good'.

However, he needn't have worried; there were plenty of jobs available in those days, and he very quickly found work in a cement factory making paving slabs. Although just five foot seven, he was powerfully built and had all the attributes for the heavy demanding work. He never turned down any overtime, which was plentiful.

He described to me the conditions of the lodgings he shared with ten or more other men, in a house that was basically a two-up, two-down. The house, a mid-terraced property, with its peeling wallpaper, damp walls, outside toilet, and no bath, had clearly seen better days. The men slept two or three to a bed, and sometimes the same bed was used again by those who had been working the night shift. If more new arrivals turned up, extra mattresses were thrown on the floor for them. Yet, there were no complaints from anyone; it was the cheapest and the best way to save money. Their conditions here, compared to the ones they were used to, were a luxury.

Most of the men were married, but none of them had their families with them. Those fortunate enough to have saved enough money moved out, buying a house of their own before calling their families over. For many Asians of that generation, there was a lack of permanency; as soon as they had made enough money, they'd be going back to their home country, or so they thought. Furthermore, many also faced discrimination from the locals, which only served to fuel their feeling of being temporary visitors.

After working for three years, my father's desire to go 'home' started to become a distant dream. Although he was doing as much overtime as he could, it seemed he was never going to make enough money to return home. Like many of his fellow countrymen, his thoughts turned instead to bringing his family to this country. He managed to save enough money and, together with a friend, bought his first house, 19 Wellington Street, Oxford—our first home here.

Having bought the house, both my father and his friend, Mr Younas Butt, called over their families. In November 1965, my mother and I, along with Mr Butt's family, came to England. I was nine years old.

My mother

During the three year-period of my father's absence from Pakistan, life suddenly became extremely difficult for my mother.

My mother had previously been married to my father's elder brother, who died soon after the marriage. As she was not one of the extended family, she was treated as an outsider and disliked. When she married my father, this increased even more.

Whilst my father was at home, everyone kept their views about her to themselves. But my father being away in England presented the perfect opportunity for some to make her life quite uncomfortable. Without my father, she had nobody to protect her, except perhaps my father's youngest brother, Uncle Ali Ahmed. However, in our culture, very few stood up against their elders. It was accepted that Ali Ahmed (he was always called by his full name for some reason) would not confront his older brother Mohammed Rakhman, who had taken an instant dislike to my mother from day one. Whilst my father was at home, he didn't dare show his true feelings. In fact, he never said a word—this in a culture where domestic violence within the marriage was the norm; even beating one's sister-in-law was accepted. With my father now in England, Uncle Rakhman saw his opportunity to make my mother's life a misery. He knew my mother would never tell her husband or anyone else; she felt it would only bring shame on the family, the main reason many women put up with their 'hand of fate'.

Reflecting on this from time to time, I often wonder why he would treat my mother like that. I can only guess at some of the reasons. Perhaps he too did not like his brother marrying a widower; he too blamed her for the death of her children. I also think he may have been a little jealous of my father's popularity, and he may have wanted the opportunity to come to England.

I never saw Uncle Rakhman attack my mother physically, only shouting at her. I recall one incident that made it clear he did not like me either. I would have been about five or six years old; it took place on our farm. It was lunchtime, and my mother had brought food for all of us, which either she or one of the other women did every day. I usually did not spend much time on the farm. But on that occasion, I was there looking after my goat.

I was in the nearest field to the farm building playing with my goat, and I came running as soon as I could smell the food. The freshly baked flatbread, or 'chapattis', and the strong smell of the lentil and vegetable curry was alluring. Meat was something we only had as a treat on special occasions like Eid or when someone came to visit.

By the time my two uncles had arrived to eat, I had just broken a piece of bread and was about to dip it into my bowl of curry, when Uncle Rakhman shouted at my mother, 'Why don't you teach that brat some manners? Does he not know he should wait for the elders to eat first?' I remember the most terrifying scowl on his face and the most frightening glare in his eyes. He then knocked the bread and bowl of curry out of my hands. My mother, fighting back tears, led me away, reassuring me we would eat later. I don't recall much else about the incident, apart from sobbing my heart out as I was led away and soothed to sleep, still hungry.

Of course, at the time, I could not understand my uncle's behaviour, especially when my mother was always telling me to think kindly of others. I could not help but think of him as the meanest person in the world. As an adult, when I think about that incident and all the other times I saw him shouting at my mother, I try to search for reasons for his behaviour and have gone from hating him to trying to understand his behaviour. I'm no psychologist, but I do believe he was genuinely outraged at the idea of children eating before adults—a bit like leaving the dining table without asking permission here. Maybe he believed that working men should eat first, as they need the nourishment to provide for the rest of the family.

My mother went through a very difficult time when my siblings died. When she lost her first child, there was some sympathy and support for her. But when she lost her second child, there was the occasional 'tut-tut' throughout the village. Unfortunately, as she lost her third child, people began to blame her for their deaths. Finally, when my mother lost her fourth child, the family and even some of the village elders told my father that there was obviously something wrong with her; perhaps she was 'cursed'. He should throw her out. They tried to persuade my father to divorce her, telling him there would be no shame in that at all. However, to my father's credit, he refused to listen to them and stayed loyal to my mother.

My parents were overjoyed when I was born. However, as mentioned previously, I was always ill. My illnesses gave some people enough of a reason to start talking to my father again, telling him to leave his wife, again trying to fill his head with the notion that she was cursed. But according to my mother, he would hear none of it, telling everyone that, while his son was alive, he would concentrate on him and do everything possible to help his survival. I believe this was another reason he brought us to England, so that I would have a better chance of survival.

It would be fair to say that my mother, privately, was quite concerned about what might have happened had I not survived. In her final months, I tried to encourage my mother to talk about some aspects of her life. However, she would only say, 'God sends us various tests in life; we only learn about the strength of our character through how we cope with these tests. A path was created for me to travel in, and with your father's support, I have travelled it.'

I took this to mean that she believed that, through culture, tradition, and religion, there is a certain way for Pakistani women to live, and there is little they can do about it. With a glint in her eyes, she added, 'Despite what it was like for me in Pakistan, look how Allah Tallah' (God) 'has provided for us now.' She sounded contented.

Mahmood Ahmed

I've always thought of my parents as a couple devoted to each other, without the open display of devotion you see from couples in England. There is a world of difference between the two cultures when it comes to how such things are thought of and displayed.

My biggest failing and regret has been my failure to find a way of telling and showing my parents the immense respect and love I have for them both.

Chapter 3

So, This Is England!

There haven't been too many things in my life I have been certain about. However, since my father was chosen to come to England, following in his footsteps was something I always felt certain about. The day he left for England I began to have reoccurring dreams about it; yet having to wait three years felt like an eternity. I was always waiting for my mother to say she had finally received a letter inviting us to join him.

Then suddenly, it came; my mother got the letter I had been praying for. Despite knowing nothing about England, I could not contain my excitement. For days, I hardly slept. I remember my mother warning me not to get too excited, for Allah Tallah may take away our good news. It was her way of helping me to remain modest and not get carried away.

I could tell, even though she hid her feelings, more for the family's sake than anything else, that deep down, she too was happy.

Along with my mother and I, my cousin, Mohammed Zaman, also came to England. My father saw an opportunity to help our extended family and adopted Zaman as his son.

***

Zaman, about five years older than me, only spent a year at school here before starting work. In Oxford, he worked as a waiter in an Indian restaurant, and then later, he worked in the textile industry, a field he stayed in for the rest of his working life. The only other thing I remember about Zaman is that he loved playing volleyball in Pakistan, and he was exceptionally good at it. Unfortunately, he never played it in England, or any other sport for that matter. Due to our age difference, we hardly spent any time in each other's company, and I never got to know him well.

Although my mother and I were both over the moon about coming to England, the rest of my father's family and even the village elders were not so pleased. They felt it was all right for men to go to England, to work, but it was wrong for women and children to do so, since women and children would be 'easily influenced' by the free and liberal Western culture. They believed that a culture that encouraged men and women to mix openly was not good for our way of life.

They were completely wrong with their concerns about my mother. The near fifty years or so in this country did little to change her outlook on life. She remained as much a Pakistani and a devout Muslim here as she ever was in Pakistan—perhaps a little happier. She hardly went out, except to visit close family or friends, and she could not speak a word of English. She never felt the need to learn English; my father or I could interpret for her if necessary. She had no need to go to the doctors or the hospital until much later in life, due to ill health—by which time her grandchildren took care of her, accompanying her to the doctors and the hospital for any appointments.

As for their concerns about me, they could not have known how right they would be. Their fears and concerns would prove to be prophetic, as you will read later.

***

It was time to get the relevant paperwork sorted out for our journey to England. The way this worked was that you knew somebody who knew somebody who was familiar with the formal process, helping you to obtain all the appropriate documentation. This usually meant a little 'greasing of palms' here and there. But quite frankly, that was hardly something that occupied my mind; grown-ups dealt with that stuff.

England was all I could think of; I wondered endlessly what it would be like. In my father's letters, there was no mention of England. He basically conveyed a set of instructions for my grandmother for how to distribute the money and to make sure I went to school. He also sent some money for my mother, some of which she saved. She gave some to my grandmother, and whatever was left, she gave to the poor.

Having the documentation sorted out, our journey towards England began when my uncle Ali Ahmed accompanied us to a nearby village, where we spent the night with Mr Butt's young family—his wife, and their daughter and son, six and four, respectively.

In the morning we were taken to the airport in Mangla by Mrs Butt's family, flying from there to Karachi. During the flight, I remember feeling excited and terrified both at the same time. The plane rattled so badly it felt as if it was going to explode. I don't know how it made it to Karachi. Having travelled to Pakistan several times since 1965, thankfully, aeroplanes have improved considerably.

In Karachi, we spent a night with my Aunt Farzand, my father's youngest sister, and her family. Mr Butt's family booked themselves into a hotel.

Early next morning, we were met at the airport by Mr Butt's family. However, as I was not used to wearing shoes, I kept slipping and sliding on the clean, shiny floor, having to hang on tightly to my uncle's hand.

The flight from Karachi to Heathrow was a complete blur, until I stepped off the plane at Heathrow airport. Autumn was reaching the end, and I was greeted by what felt like arctic conditions. I was wearing a smart suit and a jumper, but they were totally inadequate for the weather. By the time I had walked off the plane and into the airport building, I was frozen.

No matter how much I was looking forward to being in England or how excited I was about finally getting here, nothing had prepared me for the British weather! It was grey and wet; the bitterly cold wind just cut right through you. I think they call it 'the lazy wind'—it doesn't go around you; it goes through you. It left me chilled to the bone.

Several months later, my father told me a story about when he came to pick us up from the airport. He'd never learned to drive, so he asked one of his friends to go with him. In those days, very few of the locals had cars; an Asian with a car was rarer still. Anyway, once they arrived at the airport, his friend asked my father how he could recognise his family. My father's reply was, 'Oh, you won't miss my son. You will recognise him by his ears. He has jumbo ears.' Another example of my father's sense of humour. Thanks, Dad!

When we got home, there was a special meal waiting for us, a chicken curry. As it happens, I only had a few mouthfuls before throwing up. I'm not sure whether it was the food, my overexcitement, or the wonderful British weather!

Within a short period of being here, I noticed some differences in my new surroundings and environment. For example, coal was delivered door to door. I had never seen coal in Pakistan; there, the children had to go out and find wood to burn, or more likely, cow dung and horse manure, which was plentiful. When I first saw the men delivering coal, I didn't realise they were white, as they were completely covered in black soot.

I also found it strange to see the milkman deliver milk in glass bottles every morning. I had assumed children got up early each morning to milk a cow, as they did in Pakistan.

Not being the most observant of children, I usually only noticed things right in front of me. If I had been more observant, I would have noticed other differences too, such as buildings, houses, parks, gardens, buses and trains, the clothes people wore, the food they ate, and that they used cutlery. I'd have seen how polite and how happy they seemed to be, smiling when they greeted you. Unfortunately, I was far too worried about how others saw me, rather than noticing these things. When your mind is preoccupied with what others think of you or focused on not making mistakes, looking foolish, or drawing attention, you end up missing out on other things around you. Noticing things is something I learned to do much later in life.

Without making excuses for myself, a combination of these factors has had a hugely limiting effect on many areas of my life—my ability to study; to socialise and make friends; to set goals for myself; to be ambitious, driven, and motivated; and even to be comfortable in holding conversations. It became a vicious cycle, pushing me further into my shell.

***

As I now look back on when we came to England, I can't help but wonder how it must be for those coming to settle here in more recent times. Many of those who came in the fifties and sixties, including my parents, were invited here due to shortage of labour. Times have changed; today's migrants are made to feel uninvited, unwelcome, and unwanted. All who come to these shores face many challenges, particularly discrimination. This is especially so during difficult economic times—with jobs and housing scarce and with education, health, and other services stretched to the limit.

Unfortunately, political unrest and economic strife in developing countries will always push people to seek a better life in other countries, inevitably increasing immigration to countries like the United Kingdom.

Our first house

The first house my father and Mr Butt bought was not just for the eight of us. There was also a tenant. The two families shared the mortgage but still needed the rent from a tenant. Therefore, one of the downstairs rooms was rented out.

When I say 'mortgage', I don't mean it in the normal sense of borrowing money over a fixed period from the bank. Rather, several families within our community, known as 'the committee' paid a monthly sum into a pool—the total accumulated once all members had contributed the agreed amount. Members took turns taking the committee funds in a rotation that was flexible, depending on whose need was the greatest.

Occasionally, although rarely, the committee funds rolled over to the next month; sometimes, the pool was even allowed to roll over for several months, say for those buying a house. The number of families involved and the amount they paid into the committee determined the size of the committee fund. A lot of Pakistanis still use this system, due to their religious beliefs, as they are forbidden to pay or receive interest to or from a bank. Gradually this practice has decreased, with more and more Muslims using mainstream banks and due to increased numbers of Muslim banks providing interest-free services.

Our lodger

As I recall, our tenant was tall and had a beard, and he looked old to me—maybe in his forties. Well, everybody is old to a child! He was from an African Caribbean background; I only mention this as I'd never seen anyone like him before.

During the day, we hardly ever saw him; he got up early in the morning and was at work before any of the children were up. He never had any visitors. However, in the evenings, once or twice a week, he liked to have a drink. Unfortunately, when he drank, he played his music loud, and he also sang. Sometimes we could hear him banging on the doors and walls or furniture being knocked over. Incredibly, in the mornings, he just got up and went to work as if nothing had happened. To this day, I've wondered if he ever remembered anything about the previous night. This went on for several months, and it terrified me and the two Butt children. It got so frightening that, eventually, Mrs Butt asked my father to ask him to leave, which my father reluctantly did.

To his credit, our lodger left without any protest.

When I look back on that experience, I now understand the impact it had on me and the perception it created about alcohol and pubs. For years, I was terrified of going into a pub, as I thought they were full of drunks spoiling for a fight.

Today, although I have a much better understanding of pubs, clubs, and those who frequent them, what I see in most city centres is not that far removed from that early perception.

My first school

Within days of landing on British soil, I was attending school—not something I expected to happen so quickly. Despite being incredibly shy and unable to speak a word of English, I really began to enjoy school.

St Barnabas Primary School, on Hart Street, was not far from where I lived. To my shame, I don't remember any of my teachers' names. What struck me about my school was its cleanliness—a proper concrete and brick building with a solid roof, not like the semi-collapsed building with leaky roofs I was used to in Pakistan. This school had lots of different classrooms, and all the rooms had desks and chairs. I was used to sitting on dirty, muddy floors in large rooms shared by up to four different classes. The noise of so many children in one room did little for my already poor concentration levels, making it easy for me to be distracted. Here, all the children were clean and smartly dressed, and they had their own desks.

After the first few days, when I did not dare look up, I noticed that most of the children were staring at me. I couldn't figure out why; occasionally, I even caught the teacher looking. However, I felt no malice from any of them, despite what happened when, one day, a group of boys decided to follow me home.

I was about two hundred yards from the school when I heard them running towards me. As they ran past, one of them stopped and, to my horror and shock, punched me in the stomach. Being the softy I was, I doubled over in pain, trying desperately not to cry.

What happened next shocked me even more; it was something I will never forget. The boy who had just punched me was about to run off after his mates. He suddenly stopped. Amazingly, he turned round and walked back to me. He saw me wincing, doubled up with pain. I thought he was going to hit me again. To my sheer bewilderment, he simply said, 'I'm sorry. I'm sorry. I didn't think you would feel pain.'

The pain did not seem as bad as the shock of what I had just heard. I honestly didn't know whether to cry or laugh!

They say God works in mysterious ways. As it turned out, this boy and I became firm friends after that incident—just as well, as he was cock of the school. No one dared to pick on me because of our friendship and that bizarre incident.

I've reflected on this event with those boys and a later incident at a school in West Yorkshire many times. Both had a big influence on my attitude and response to discrimination, particularly racism, later in life. Those incidents helped me think differently about people's behaviour; I wanted to understand people's motivation for carrying out such acts and not simply label them. My view is that those who carry out acts of discrimination do so, overall, due to ignorance and sometimes, as was the case with these boys, out of curiosity. With others, it is often their own insecurity or fear of the unknown that leads them to lash out, ridicule, or attack those who are different. Of course, there are always those who just cannot accept any form of difference.

Mahmood Ahmed

'I am here to teach you English'

As I take myself back to my childhood in Oxford, I recall a sense of calm and quiet that I now associate with those times.

At the time, I had no idea that Oxford was one of, if not the greatest seats of learning in the world. Having lived there, and despite my lack of academia, it makes me proud just to have some sort of connection with it. However, while I was living there, the university set up a project to teach English to children of all immigrant families. A second-year history undergraduate called Richard—strange how I remember his name—came to our house every Thursday evening for about an hour to teach me the alphabet, the times table, and how to put some sentences together.

On one occasion, after Richard had finished teaching me, I managed to persuade him to have something to eat with me. I remember it as if it happened only yesterday. My mum had made my favourite curry dish, *keema* (mincemeat), with potatoes and peas. She laid the food—curry, chapattis, some salad, and a jug of water with two glasses—on the table for us and left the room. I should have taken the lead and shown Richard how to eat an Indian meal. But because I hesitated, Richard took the whole chapatti (roti, as we call it) and tried to get some keema on it. He failed comically, with the keema falling all over the table.

After both of us laughed at his attempt, I broke off a small piece of chapatti and used it to scoop a small amount of keema onto it before putting it in my mouth. Richard followed suit. Unfortunately, he had never had any kind of spicy food before. As soon as it hit his mouth, he went bright red, picked up the jug of water, and gulped half of it down as quickly as he could. The curry nearly blew his head off! I just couldn't contain myself and broke out in hysterics. It is one of my funniest childhood memories of Oxford. Richard, to his credit, also saw the funny side; not only did he have some more keema and roti, he developed a real taste for Indian food and looked forward to my mum's cooking every week.

From what I recall of Richard, he was an incredibly patient young man. I remember struggling to pronounce unfamiliar verbs and nouns, particularly words beginning with 'v' and 'w', always getting them mixed up. Yet Richard never got cross or shouted. The way he dealt with my mistakes was a new experience. I was used to a clout round the ears when I got things wrong at school in Pakistan.

That was the only time as a child I felt comfortable about learning. And I started to progress well, reading just as well as the other children in my class and became better than most in maths.

Thank you, Richard, for all that you did for me.

The wonderful English people

Perhaps when people talk about 'British values', they should remind themselves of some of the 'old-fashioned' values, based on thinking of others first. In Oxford, my father told me about the wonderful local people and their kindness.

Apart from the man who walked with him to the address on his piece of paper, my father told me about a time when a dropped wallet in the street would probably still be there or handed in at a police station. What are the chances of that today? I realise of course there is always an element of exaggeration, but those values and others such as a sense of fair play, standing up for the underdog, or standing against any kind of injustice were much more prevalent in England in those days and much admired by people who came to live here.

Why have we allowed such values to erode?

Muslim-Sikh friendship

It was in Oxford that my father struck up a lifelong friendship with Mr Balbir Singh, from India, who most Pakistanis would have called the 'enemy'. The two men had met at work, and after we moved into our house, Mr Singh and his family would often visit. My father greeted them in Punjabi, with great warmth, and Mr Singh responded with equal joviality. It was wonderful to see how their faith never interfered with their friendship. Mr Singh had twin boys of similar age to me. However, from the ages of five, their father had gotten them interested in boxing, and they took to it like ducks to water. They would often bring their boxing gloves with them and spar with each other for us. This delighted my father, for he loved boxing. When the 'greatest', Muhammad Ali, was on television, my father would find someone with a TV set and stay up until the early hours of the morning to watch. I also know that he secretly wished I had taken up boxing. Unfortunately, another great British sport was to take my fancy, one he did not initially care for.

The friendship between my father and Mr Singh continued to grow, until we moved from Oxford to Bradford, a couple of years later. However, it was rekindled again when we moved to Blackburn, in the mid-seventies, where Mr Singh and his family had resettled. Their friendship only ended when, sadly, Mr Singh passed away.

However, the same could not be said for me and Mr Singh's twins; we never really became friends and went our separate ways as adults.

Chapter 4

Smoke Chimneys and Cotton Mills: Our Move 'Up North'

Aunt Muzambil: A remarkable woman

Life for all the family seemed to be going well in Oxford. I was enjoying going to school, even though I mainly kept myself to myself. I really looked forward to Richard's visits every Thursday. Without realising it, Richard was becoming my guiding elder brother. There were no further unpleasant incidents of any kind at school. If anything, all the other children showed a friendly interest in me. My father had a good job, and my mum and Mr Butt's wife seemed to have built a good relationship between them, despite coming from two different upbringings—my mother an uneducated rural housewife, Mrs Butt city-educated and sophisticated. We were all happy and content with our new life.

Being the pessimist that I was, I always felt, for some reason, it was not going to last. And so it proved.

Mahmood Ahmed

We had been in Oxford for about a year and half when my mother received some news about her youngest sister. Aunt Muzambil, along with her husband, Fazal, and their four children, Kulsum, Akhtar, Asghar, and Zainab, had settled in Bradford. Lots of people from the Mirpur area of Pakistan had settled either in Bradford or in the West Midlands, around Birmingham.

Poor Aunt Muzambil was only in her late twenties when she was diagnosed with cancer. As soon as my mother found out, she asked my father if we could move to Bradford. My father agreed without hesitation; we moved to Yorkshire in 1967.

Bradford was so different from Oxford, the place that I had instantly fallen in love with. Bradford was huge—busier; noisier; and, I hate to say, dirtier than Oxford. Luckily for me, these initial thoughts about Bradford didn't last long. I soon began to adapt to my new surroundings, with a little help from my cousins, especially Akhtar, with whom I had a close bond from my visits to Dadyal.

There were many things I didn't know about Bradford or Yorkshire—the strong cotton industry; the unique way Yorkshire's cricketers were selected, only those born in the county; the beauty of the Yorkshire Dales; the Brontë sisters and Haworth; and, of course, the way they speak in those parts.

Initially, we stayed with my aunt and her family in a massive three-storey house on Hanover Square, not far from the city centre. The house was big, but beautiful it wasn't. The paintwork was flaky, the wallpaper was peeling off, and all the furniture and fittings had seen better days. I can't remember it having a garden, although I guess it must have had at least a backyard of some sort. Despite the condition of the house, I was excited to be with my cousins.

My father had no problem finding a job in one of the cotton mills, and very soon, he was able to buy a house of his own, a three-storey end-terraced property on Arnold Place (number 18).

Shortly afterwards, my aunt's family also sold their house and moved into a mid-terraced property (number 15) on our street. Both houses were a step up from the previous property we'd shared.

Soon after moving to our new house, two of my cousins from Pakistan came to live with us. Liaqat Mahmood, who later got the nickname George (the one who fell off the donkey with me), and my future wife's eldest brother, Amjid. There was plenty of room in our new house, which had two large living rooms; a backyard; a three-piece bathroom in the attic (a real luxury in those days); a big cellar, where we had our kitchen; three bedrooms on the first floor; and a further, exceptionally large bedroom in the attic, used by George, Amjid, and me. Zaman had his own room.

My mum used to make enough food to feed an army, and the only chores the three of us younger boys had to do each morning was to get the fire in the living room going. We all hated doing that. To get it going, we'd twist a sheet of newspaper around before lighting it from the cooker and then place it in the fireplace with some coal and other pieces of cardboard and newspapers. We had to keep blowing until the cardboard caught fire, which in turn slowly lit the coal. We'd then blow on the flames for several minutes to get them going, fighting to keep the smoke out of our eyes. This was before we discovered firelighters, which made the whole process so much easier. The fire would then be covered up by a metal sheet to get the flames going. Once we heard the flames roaring, the metal sheet was removed, allowing us to enjoy the heat.

***

Having now been in Bradford for nearly three months, I hadn't seen anything visibly wrong with my aunt, and I began to wonder why we had to move. It was the early days of her diagnosis; apart from some pain, she showed few other symptoms. But very soon she became terribly ill. Within weeks, she was bedridden and began to suffer horrific pains in her legs and lower back. I often heard her cry out in agony. I could not imagine the pain she was in, and her suffering made me feel terribly guilty about my selfish thoughts.

Her pain and what she went through was something I only came to recognise when my son Bashir was diagnosed with bowel cancer many years later. To her credit, although she couldn't help crying out, I never heard her say, 'Why me, God?' But watching her suffer like that didn't stop me asking God, *why her? Why put someone so kind and caring through this?* I didn't get any answers.

In Pakistan, I'd become quite close to Aunt Muzambil, closer than I was to any of my relatives. It was this closeness to her that led me to question God. Of all the people I knew, she was the kindest and the bravest. Whether in England or in Pakistan, she was the only one who would ask me about school and about my friends and hobbies— something not even my parents did.

Looking back, Aunt Muzambil was quite clearly a woman ahead of her time—certainly not your typical uneducated woman from a rural Pakistani village. Unlike most Pakistani women, she'd question most things—even what her husband or family said, making most of the household decisions. Talking to the children about small things, the things that mattered, came naturally to her. She was the only one who openly showed her emotions and told us how precious we were. She would make us laugh and give us all a bit of pocket money. I don't know where she got it from, but it seemed as if she always had some for the children. The more I think about her, the more remarkable she appears.

Fifty years or so on, we are only just beginning to see some Pakistani women take the lead within their households and act as equals to men. My aunt was doing it back then—not consciously taking up the struggle for women but just being herself, strong and determined. She had her detractors, of course, family members and other men in the community who questioned her behaviour, but she was undeterred by it all. Whenever I used to visit her in Dadyal as a child, she'd made me feel so special, telling me that all the children in our extended family were my brothers and sisters, as I didn't have any of my own. I often wished she lived closer to Kala Gujran.

Aunt Muzambil's kindness towards me deepened my guilt for not being able to bring her relief from her suffering. That was the only time I wished I was a doctor; perhaps then I may have found a way to save her. After her death, I felt I had lost the only person I ever felt close to.

My memories of Aunt Muzambil will always be of someone who was able to show warmth and affection without worrying about what anyone else thought. The few times I saw her in Dadyal, she was able to comfort me in a different way to my mother. I feel somewhat disloyal by admitting this, and you may get the impression that my mother didn't care for me. She did, in her own unique way, and I cannot ever question her devotion to me; but she was unable to do it in quite the way her younger sister could.

As I reflect, I understand the reasons my mother could not do that. As well as her unique personality, Aunt Muzambil grew up within her own family environment, married someone from her extended family, and always felt part of the bigger extended family. So, she grew to be herself. In contrast, my mother, after marrying young, had no one from her family around her and spent a lot of time among people who didn't want or like her. It was inevitable that she'd learn to suppress her feelings and emotions.

Meanwhile, losing Aunt Muzambil knocked me further into my shell, making expressing myself even more difficult.

Comics and sweets

When I was in Oxford, I don't ever remember going to the local corner shop. In fact, I don't even remember a corner shop near where we lived. In Bradford, the corner shop was handily placed at the end of our street where it joined Whitley Hill. Like most Pakistani children I knew, I wasn't allowed to buy sweets, but occasionally the adults would buy them as a treat for us. Reading comics was out of the question. Most Pakistani parents felt that reading fictional stories wasn't good for us. However, it didn't stop us—not even a goody two shoes like me!

I'd buy them and hide them among my books in my school bag, where I knew my mum would never look. Even if she did, she'd probably assume they were magazines from school.

Usually, I only bought one a week, and if I had any money left over, I would occasionally treat myself to *The Beano*. But my favourite comic was *The Amazing Spiderman*. I was so drawn to the character of Peter Parker, who, like me, was lonely and often sad. Becoming Spiderman allowed him to escape to another world, where he would be transformed, helping society fight the bad guys—something I would always dream of, but maybe not the fighting bit!

I still love all the Marvel comic characters and watch all the latest films, which often attracts a quizzical look from the woman in my life. 'You are still such a little boy,' she will say. I can't argue with that.

Reading in general, whether comics or books, is not something I've managed to pass on to Mehboob and Bashir; neither have been avid readers. Fortunately, in recent years, both have started reading.

Once I'd discovered the art of breaking rules, I moved on to the more serious crime of … buying sweets. My favourites were Black Jacks and Fruit Salads, soft and chewy. Just thinking about them makes my mouth water!

My first friend

In Bradford, I formed my first lifelong friendship, with Abdul Hamid Anjum, or Hamid as we called him.

Hamid and I met at Belle Vue Boys Grammar School and played football together in the nearby Drummond School, near to me—made famous many years later by the school's head teacher, who wrote a critical article on multiculturalism and its effect on British education.

Hamid was the nearest thing I had to having my own brother, despite him being a Chelsea fan! When I used to tease him about supporting a southern team, he would simply say, 'You've room to talk, supporting one from the other side of the Pennines!' It was a cardinal sin to support the team from Lancashire. I'm proud to say our friendship has stood the test of time, although now, due to our busy lives, we see less of each other than we'd like. It was with him and my other lifelong friend, Ossy, that the idea of going on day trips with our families first came about, many years later.

As children, Hamid and I were always at each other's houses, pretending to be studying or eating meals together. Although I was slightly older than Hamid, he was always much more aware of himself and his surroundings, more 'streetwise', more outgoing, and better-looking too. He knew what I was like, yet he warmed to me and won my trust, which could not have been easy.

We always kept in touch after my family moved to Lancashire, our families becoming close with regular visits to each other's homes.

Memories from Bierley Church Junior School, Bradford

When we moved from Oxford to Bradford, a place at my new school, Bierley Church Junior School (now East Bierley Primary School) was ready and waiting for me within days of our arrival. This school was located much further than my school in Oxford—over five miles from where I lived. Each morning, I walked a short distance to Green Lane and caught a free bus to school. The bus had a small board with a blue circle displayed at the front so that children got on the right bus, as there were several other buses going to different schools, displaying different coloured shapes.

I was the only Asian in my class; in fact, I was only one of three non-white children in the school.

As it was a Church of England school, each morning started with every class saying the Lord's Prayer. Although I didn't know the prayer, I would close my eyes, bow my head, and say my own prayer. I never told my parents about having to say a pray each morning, as I always thought they'd be upset with me reciting a prayer from another religion. To this day, I don't know whether that would have been the case or whether it was something I convinced myself of.

I remember a playtime game, which led to a friendship with a boy called Mark. Just like my friend at St Barnabas in Oxford, Mark was cock of the school. Again, I'd landed on my feet.

The game was called 'catch and kiss'. It was a simple game; boys and girls took it in turns to run off and hide and then wait to be caught. The first one to catch a girl or a boy got to kiss them. I'm not sure I should be admitting this, but I desperately wanted to play the game. But in my culture, boys and girls were forbidden to play with each other; on top of that, I was, of course, far too shy to even look at a girl, let alone kiss one.

Mark was hugely popular with all the children, and there was not a girl in the whole school who didn't fancy him. But because of his friendship with me, Mark stopped playing the game too, for a while anyway. Although none of the children said anything to me, they knew it was because of me. Shortly afterwards, I told Mark that I was happy for him to start playing again and that I'd just watch. This pleased everyone.

Mark also taught me to play marbles, the English way, as well as hopscotch.

First fight

A further memory from this school that stands out is of my one and only fight, both as a schoolboy and as an adult.

I'm the first to admit I was never the bravest of boys; however, I did manage to get myself involved in standing up for things that were either wrong or unjust. Later, this would be one reason I chose a certain career path. If the truth be known, I've always been fearful of any kind of violence, but a sense of morality takes over when I see injustice.

On this occasion at school, before I knew it, I was in the middle of a fight. You know how things sometimes happen in life and you don't have time to think, so you just react? There's a voice inside that tells us, *enough is enough. Do something!* This happens even to the most placid among us. Anyway, I had what you might call a 'George McFly moment', from the film *Back to the Future*.

In the film, if you haven't seen it, George is Marty McFly's father. Marty is the main character. George is the kind of man who avoids any sort of conflict or confrontation and does his best to placate others to an embarrassing level—that is, until one day he sees Biff and the woman he secretly loves in Biff's car. He sees Biff making advances that she is desperately resisting, which Biff ignores. George opens the car door, and while Biff is flabbergasted that he is even there, George knocks him clean out with just one punch, a punch carrying a great deal of anger and supressed emotion.

And so, it was with me. I saw this boy picking on a few of the smaller children on the playground. He started to push one of them, aggressively. The smaller boy looked terrified. I was with a group of children, including Mark. We all saw what was happening. We thought Mark would jump in and stop him, but for some reason, he didn't; perhaps it was the boy's size.

Anyway, the terrified look on the little boy's face became too much for me to bear, and I reacted, which surprised everyone, including myself. Hoping I wouldn't be heard, I muttered, 'Why don't you leave him alone?' sort of under my breath.

Well, he turned towards me and, in an instant, had me by the scruff of my collar. He was about to punch me when, instinctively, I headbutted him, catching him flush on the nose. He fell backwards, dazed, landing on his backside, probably more out of shock than pain.

Outwardly, I managed to remain calm, but inside, I was shaking like a leaf, finding it extremely difficult not to throw up.

What I had done was completely out of character and totally unexpected. However, everyone around me started cheering and jumping with joy, slapping me on the shoulders. For that moment, I had become a hero (just like Spiderman) and everyone's friend. But as I looked at the boy on the ground, all alone and no one going towards him, I felt sorry for him.

Our paths never crossed again. He simply got up, walked away, and became sort of non-existent after that. If we did come across each other, at playtime or dinnertime, he would simply look away or turn and walk the other way. During PE lessons, when we played team sports, he would be the last to be picked.

Even though what he did was wrong, I felt as if what I had done was even worse. That boy was from an African Caribbean background, the only one in the school. In doing the 'right' thing, I had now isolated him from all the other children. When I think back to the incident now, I feel saddened by it, often asking myself, what if he was behaving that way to protect himself? Being the only black kid at the school, maybe he picked on others so he wouldn't be picked on himself. I must admit, it's one of those things I wish I could have done more about or that the outcome could have been different.

A Hindu, a Muslim, and a Hamster

My final memory from this school involved another Asian boy, who joined my class a few months after me. He was called Shantilal and was a Hindu from India.

I have already mentioned the conflict between India and Pakistan following partition. Both Shantilal and I had been brought up in an environment where we had been told how inhumanely the other side had behaved, building up a terrifying picture of hatred for the other side. I clearly remember everyone around me telling me how barbaric the Indian people were—that they would attack our villages and kill our women and children without mercy. They were not human, and it was the duty of every Pakistani to kill them.

It's little wonder that, having grown up around so much hatred for the Indian people, I had brought these hateful feelings with me to this country. And it was the same for Shantilal. These feelings had remained dormant from the moment I had left Pakistan until the day Shantilal walked into my classroom; seeing each other for the first time, we instantly became sworn enemies.

When I first saw him, I remembered all I'd been told about the Indian people, the resentment and anger flooding back. I felt pure hatred for him, and when I looked into his eyes, his feelings were evidently just as fierce. I knew that, if we had an opportunity to be alone and if we could, we would 'knock seven bells' out of each other. For those first three months, we simply glared at each other.

These feelings only came to an end following a bizarre incident, which involved our teacher and her pet hamster. One day, she had brought the pet into the classroom for us. Unfortunately, the poor thing somehow managed to get out of its cage and get lost. The teacher paired the children up to search for her hamster. And yes, in her wisdom, she paired Shantilal with me.

What happened next is something I still struggle to fully understand and find hard to put into words. Why or how our feelings towards each other changed so dramatically that instant is one of those things that is difficult to explain. Up to that point, we had looked at each other only to confirm our loathing. But this time, when I looked up at Shantilal, something inside me changed. For some reason, this time, I didn't see the Indian boy I hated so much. I only saw a boy who, more than anyone else in the class, looked like me—shy and alone.

He had brown skin, jet black greasy hair, and an expression that said he was uncertain about his surroundings. For the first time, I realised he had more in common with me than anyone else in the class. So I asked myself, *Why do I hate him so much?* A nervous smile broke out across my lips, and to my great relief, he smiled back. After that, not only did Shantilal find the hamster, much to our teacher's relief, but the two of us also became close friends.

We never told our parents about our friendship, as we didn't know how they would react. We were terrified they may try to end it.

I now understand why we initially hated each other. Those feelings were the product of our environment, our surroundings, and what was drummed into us. While I was growing up in Pakistan, all those factors came together to create a hateful picture of the Indian people.

Although I didn't realise it at the time, moving to England and meeting Shantilal helped to change my feelings and attitude towards the Indian people and, gradually, my understanding of those different from me.

It's such a pity, as advanced as modern society has become, that we continue to struggle to learn to live peacefully with others, irrespective of difference. Every day we see examples of many conflicts caused by intolerance all over the world.

Unfortunately, my friendship with Shantilal ended on the last day at school. We never knew where each other lived and didn't keep in touch—another example of how fear controls and restricts us.

Mahmood Ahmed

Frizinghall Junior High School

In September 1969, I went to my next school, Frizinghall Junior High on Salisbury Road.

I left behind my friends, Mark and Shantilal; this was a massive loss to me, as they were a source of reassurance and personal learning. With Mark, it was security and a feeling of envy. The security came from knowing that, because Mark was my friend, none of the white boys would pick on me. I was envious of the fact that he could, so freely, play with girls, which was off limits for me. Those simple pleasures were forbidden for Muslim children. All I could do was stand around and watch the other children enjoying themselves, while I could only dream of joining in.

With Shantilal, there was a different kind of learning. If I hadn't come to England and met him, I may never have understood difference and the damaging impact of narrow perspectives and false perceptions. I may not have become so willing to readily hear other perspectives. If I hadn't had left Pakistan, I wouldn't have discovered a world outside my little village. Fortunately, all that changed; the move allowed me to meet people different to me. Those early experiences would help me in later life to be more open-minded and more effective in my job and to look at things from other's points of view—or, as the saying goes, 'to walk in other people's shoes'.

Often, we want others to understand us, without making the effort to understand them first. This is something I regularly remind myself of, due to those early experiences.

As I reflect on my experiences, I read again and better understand Dr Martin Luther King's words, when he said, 'Darkness cannot drive out darkness: Only light can do that. Hate cannot out hate: Only love can do that.'

Frizinghall was a struggle in many ways. However, the first thing that springs to mind is that there were more Asian children at the school, although I don't remember any Asian girls. It was not the number of Asian children that added to my struggles but my background and the colour of my skin. It was here that, along with other Asian children, I had my many experiences of racism and being and seeing others attacked, just because of who we were.

These attacks were nothing like the one that had taken place in Oxford; those boys were just curious about me. Here, it was purely hatred for those with a different skin colour, not curiosity, that motivated the frequent and vicious attacks which often followed verbal abuse and taunting. These boys seemed to enjoy causing us pain and suffering, laughing and sniggering as they lashed out.

As frightening as the attacks were, we were more scared of going home and telling our parents, knowing they would only blame us for what they saw as us getting ourselves into trouble. Such attacks and incidents only further dented my already low confidence and fragile self-esteem.

Looking back, I have no doubt why those attacks took place. Rising resentments against the increasing number of immigrants, a downturn in the economy, and inflammatory and sensational media headlines all contributed.

What's even more disturbing is that the school and our teachers did nothing to help. All the attacks took place on school premises, yet the very people we should have been able to count on to make things better chose to ignore them.

As the attacks became more violent and became more frequent, a few of the braver Asian boys decided to stand up for themselves and fight back. To my shame, I was not one of them; I would take what came my way and hope the attackers would move on to another poor soul.

The logic of that thinking, when I compare it with what I did when I stood up for the smaller children at my previous school, makes no sense. Why did I stand up for the other children and not for myself? I don't know. I guess I reacted instinctively at Bierley, in a one-off situation. At Frizinghall, I had time to think about the consequences of getting involved in regular fights and getting into further trouble at home, which was much more difficult to deal with.

However, those who stood up for themselves went against their parents—parents who'd constantly drilled into us that we were to stay out of trouble, avoid getting into fights, and refrain from misbehaving at school. This was one reason there were so many well-behaved Asian children at school in those days. Nevertheless, a small number decided to fight back. But they were heavily outnumbered, so they 'tooled up', carrying flick knives, knuckledusters, even small metal bars to protect themselves.

On one occasion, when a group of English lads attacked one Asian boy, he pulled out a knife to defend himself. One of the white boys from the group ran into the school and told a teacher, who then called the police. The Asian boy was taken away by the police. It appeared as if nothing was said to the white boys; certainly nothing was said about it by the school to us. We felt neither the teachers nor the police wanted to hear our side.

Another unhappy memory from Frizinghall concerned my teacher

Mr Blackburn, who had placed some faith in me. Unfortunately, as with my parents, I let him down too.

Mr Blackburn had been working on an important document. When he'd finished, he asked me to take it down to another teacher, in one of the workshops about three hundred yards away from the main school building. It was in the middle of winter, and it had been snowing heavily. He told me to take care not to fall or drop the document. If it got wet, it would be ruined.

Lo and behold, that's exactly what happened! As I gingerly made my way to the workshop, I slipped and fell. The document, although in an envelope, ended up underneath me, as I slid down the hill on my back towards the workshop. It was completely ruined. I can still see the utter horror on Mr Blackburn's face. He didn't say a word, but the disappointment on his face said it all, punishment enough for me.

Such incidents tend to upset me more than physical punishment or pain. When people place their trust in me and I let them down, I feel their sense of disappointment immensely.

Thankfully, I have some happier memories from this school too. One of them is about two fellow pupils who stood out from the rest. Errol, a black kid, who went onto become the northern schools' boxing champion, and Abdullah, who was rather good at cricket.

Errol and I became good friends, despite it being an unusual friendship because we were so different from each other. Errol was bigger and much more muscular than me. At school he had an aggressive persona, but when we were on our own, he was relaxed and gentle. At the weekends, we regularly visited each other's homes, often eating together. As I recall, I seemed to be at his home more than he was at mine; maybe it had something to do with his pretty sister!

Stealing an occasional glance at her was as far as it went—in case you were wondering.

Errol was the only non-Pakistani boy to ever come to our house. My mum made a great deal of fuss over him, and he lapped up the attention and the food. He tried to get me interested in boxing but gave up very quickly after taking me to his gym and watching me make a fool of myself with the skipping rope.

Abdullah was a quiet boy, like me, but that was the only thing we had in common. He was an incredibly talented cricketer, able to bat, bowl, and field. On top of that, he was an outstanding athlete. He had no problems getting onto the school cricket team.

I have no doubt he had enough ability to make it into professional cricket; he was head and shoulders above anyone when it came to cricketing ability. Unfortunately, he never fulfilled his boyhood potential or his dream of playing for Yorkshire and England. Several factors probably stood in his way, including his parents' attitude towards sport and racism.

A glimpse of his talents first came to the fore when we were playing a game together during break times. The game, whose name escapes me, starts with one player chosen to be 'it'. That player had to try and hit others with a tennis ball, whilst the other players ran off, trying to avoid being hit. It was difficult at first, as you had to attempt to hit others from wherever the ball landed. If someone was hit, he became part of your team. Then you could throw the ball to each other to make it easier to hit other players. The more players who were hit, the more players ended up on your team, until everyone was hit. The last player to be hit was declared the winner. No one wanted Abdullah to be it, as he was so deadly accurate with the ball. He could hit you from any distance, at incredible speed. It really hurt when he threw the ball at you.

My next memory from this school is about falling in love, as if I knew what 'love' was back then.

We met by accident. Or was it fate? Shortly after starting at this school, we were moved into different classes based on ability. I don't remember whether I moved up to her class or she moved down to mine, but we ended up in the same class. Furthermore, our teacher, decided to change the layout of the classroom. Instead of the formal rows of desks across the room, we were put into clusters of four desks together. Each cluster had two girls and two boys. We ended up in the same cluster, sitting opposite each other. For this girl to be sat directly opposite me had to be fate, right?

I couldn't take my eyes off hers. But even if my culture and my parents had allowed it, as shy and awkward as I was, I'd never have dared to do anything else. I was so convinced I'd be rejected, telling myself no girl would waste her time on me. Those feelings of envy I experienced with Mark came back again.

As a Muslim, I went to the mosque a lot, to learn the Quran and to do my prayers. Often, there would be two other things I secretly prayed for at the end of my usual prayers. Firstly, I prayed for my beloved Manchester United's poor form to come to an end, or at least for Liverpool to stop winning. Secondly, I prayed for God to provide me with enough courage to ask a girl out. Unfortunately, neither of my prayers were answered. I always believed that the second prayer would never be answered, as it was a sin even to ask for such a thing.

Sitting so close to this girl, I found it difficult not to gaze at her. No matter how hard I tried to be discreet, there were occasions when she caught me out, and I felt extremely embarrassed, even though she never said anything. Sadly, she also never gave me any sign of encouragement either—not even a smile.

My final memory from Frizinghall involves one of our young teachers, Miss Lilly (not her real name), who taught English. As was the all the rage at the time, she used to wear a miniskirt.

Miss Lilly had gorgeous long legs, which all the boys stared at. Some did it discreetly; others were more brazen about it. Some of the daredevils went a little further. As Miss Lilly walked past their desks, they would 'accidently' drop a pencil or pen, hoping she would bend down to pick it up. She did, a couple of times, before wising up.

Even when I had the opportunity, I never dared to look, too petrified of getting caught. How did I know she had gorgeous long legs? I hear you ask. Well, all right, maybe I did peek, once or twice!

Belle Vue Boys' Grammar School

In 1971, I went to my final school in Bradford, Belle Vue Boys' Grammar School, off Toller Lane. It should have been my final school, but I'll come to that later.

By the time I started this school, the population of black and Asian people living in Britain had grown considerably, increasing the number of children from these backgrounds in schools. I'd already made my first black friend, Errol. He continued to win boxing championships at our new school, but we somehow drifted apart, until eventually we hardly saw each other at all.

I was hoping that the racist attacks we'd suffered at my previous school would not follow me to my new school. Unfortunately, they did, increasing in frequency too. The only difference here was that they were instigated, mainly, by one pupil—Terry (not his real name).

Terry was bigger and a couple of years older than most of the new children. He had cropped blond hair and used to wear black bovver boots, a long black trench coat, and red braces over a white T-shirt. He was a typical angry, snarling, spitting skinhead. I never understood why the school allowed him to get away with not wearing the school uniform. He'd terrify all Asian and black boys. Standing by the school gates, he hurled abuse at us and lashed out as we walked past. He took great pleasure in seeing the terrified look on our faces. Sometimes, when he felt less aggressive, he would just snigger and spit at us. I considered myself lucky, mostly suffering only his sniggering and spitting, perhaps the occasional kick. Some of the other Asian lads were not so lucky— Terry would chase and physically attack them or encourage members of his gang to do so, gleefully watching. There was no provocation; he seemed simply to enjoy inflicting pain.

Again, I never stood up to him or his like. However, there was one Pathan boy, Asghar (not his real name), who never backed down. No matter how much of a beating he got or how many boys he was up against, he always fought back.

Many of us had witnessed him being attacked several times, but we didn't dare go to his aid. The fear of being beaten up crippled our sense of morality. After several beatings, Asghar decided enough was enough, and out of desperation, he started carrying a little pocket-knife to protect himself. The blade was no more than two inches long. The next time he was attacked, he took it out to defend himself. Unfortunately, the only damage he inflicted was on himself. He ended up cutting his right hand as the knife closed around his fingers during his struggle with the four thugs attacking him. Worse still, when the police arrived, they arrested him for carrying an offensive weapon.

To his credit, Asghar never complained or asked for help from any of us. Yet he would never walk by whenever he saw any of us being attacked.

Since then, I've learned more about the fearless Pathan people from Pakistan and Afghanistan and their reputation for bravery. You may also be aware of how the Russians found this out, to their cost, when they invaded Afghanistan in the 1980s.

Fortunately, over the next two years or so, these racial attacks gradually subsided. Black and Asian children started to fight back and formed their own gangs, who stood up for the younger children too. The teachers reported these incidents to the police, who, rather reluctantly, began to patrol around the school. Finally, and perhaps more significantly, Terry left school.

Talking of police officers, I could never understand how they, who were supposed to uphold the law without favour or fervour, could turn a blind eye. I was to have my eyes opened many years later.

Despite the racial attacks, Belle Vue was a place where I formed special relationships with some of my teachers. The first of these was Mr Marrier, our physics teacher. He was a very gentle and mild-mannered man and always made me feel special.

One day, as we left his class, he asked everyone to open their books to make sure we'd copied everything from the board. When I went to show him mine, before I could open it, he simply said, 'Not you, Mahmood, I trust you.' I felt so proud.

In contrast, many of the other children showed little or no respect for him. They would often talk or throw things at each other while his back was turned.

Looking back now, I wonder whether it was respect that I had for him Mr Marrier or the fact that I felt sorry for him. He always found it difficult to control the class. His instructions to 'be quiet' fell on deaf ears.

I can't be sure, but it seems that, from that moment onward, earning people's trust became important to me. Many years later, as a police officer, building relationships with others was a key part of my role; and being able to earn people's trust helped immensely.

Another of the teachers I had respect for was Mr Betts, our French teacher. Mr Betts earned his respect through his fearsome reputation. He was a firm believer in corporal punishment—if you dared misbehave in his class, he wouldn't hesitate to give you 'six of the best'. Nobody ever did. Although, like the rest of the class, I feared him, I also thought he was very fair, and I don't recall ever being caned by him.

Finally, there was another teacher who I thought came to teach at the school simply because of me. With my love of football growing and him being our sports teacher, ours would be a 'dream' relationship, or so I thought.

As you know, I came to this country in November 1965, just seven months before England hosted and won the World Cup. Unfortunately, back then, we didn't have a television set, so I missed it all and didn't become hooked on football until we moved to Bradford, after watching some lads playing near where I lived. It was in Bradford my father bought a little black-and-white TV set, and I started to watch *Match of the Day*. I was instantly captivated by the magic of three of Britain's greatest players—George Best, Dennis Law, and Sir Bobby Charlton. Those of you who follow football will know that they all played for Manchester United, managed by the legendary Sir Matt Busby.

By the time I came to this school, I was well and truly hooked on football. Soon after I started at Belle Vue, this new teacher, Mr Busby, became our PE teacher. At the time, I believed he was Sir Matt's son, and he was sent specifically to coach and train me in my preparations to join Manchester United. For months, I ignored what my friends told me. I was convinced I was going to be playing for my beloved United and follow in the footsteps of my heroes, guided by Sir Matt's son.

I don't know how I thought that could ever happen. I loved playing football but played without my parents' knowledge. They didn't want me to play any kind of 'contact' sport; as I was so fragile, they feared I would be seriously hurt. However, I couldn't stop playing football, so I continued to go against their wishes, hoping they would never find out. I played during lunchtime at school and in the evenings and weekends, when I told my mum I was going to the library.

At school, I did what I could to impress our new teacher. However, it all seemed to be in vain, as I never even got an encouraging nod or word from Mr Busby. It finally began to dawn on me that, perhaps, I wasn't destined to play for United after all. It took a while for me to come to terms with the most disappointing and soul-destroying experience of my young life. My dream was completely shattered. Of course, it was only ever a dream. But for a short period of time, it was nonetheless a wonderful dream.

***

It was at this school that I was also to have my eyes opened to the fact that a small number of Asian boys and girls were now beginning to go out with each other—secretly, of course. It seemed to me that boys and girls who'd come from the cities in Pakistan, whose parents were educated and had a more liberal outlook on life, were taking risks and having relationships with each other. I couldn't believe my eyes when I came upon a Pakistani boy and girl holding hands, strolling across the school playing fields.

I thought to myself, *that takes guts. I could never do that.*

Pakistani entertainment in Bradford

Before I move on to the next chapter, I must briefly tell you what Pakistanis in Bradford did for entertainment.

For many Pakistanis, entertainment was visiting family and friends and enjoying food. However, by the late 1960s and early 1970s, major cities with large Pakistani populations like Bradford had started to see cinemas opening up, providing family entertainment. The first one was called Soldo, on Manningham Lane near the city centre; later, another one opened on Carlisle Street. This recreation outlet started off quite slowly in the Pakistani community, as there were not many Pakistani films to watch. There was still some animosity and ill feeling towards the 'Indians', particularly among the first generation, who refused to watch Indian films and would not allow their children to do so either.

Some parents didn't want their children to go to the cinema, full stop. Cinemas were for adults only. They thought such places would be bad influences on the children. Slowly this later changed, and we began to watch Pakistani films. *Farangee* was the first film I ever saw, depicting the Indo-Pak War.

As it was a Pakistani film, it naturally showed Pakistani soldiers 'bravely' holding off an attack by the massively bigger and better-equipped Indian army. It was a typical propaganda film by the Pakistani government.

After a while, we found these types of films boring and started to watch the Indian Bollywood blockbusters, which were much more exciting. This began to happen more regularly when we moved again. I've forgotten a lot of the film names, but the ones I do remember are *Mother India*; *Amar, Akbar, Anthony*; and *Sholay*—the latter two with my favourite actor, Amitabh Buchan.

Most if not all Asians films were and still are exceptionally long; full of music, singing, and dancing; and always seem to contain an element of human tragedy and suffering. Not that I am trying to put anyone off!

The only other thing I remember enjoying, other than football, was a stroll through Manningham Park, or 'Lister Park', just off Manningham Lane and about a mile and a half from our house. I loved the open green spaces and the freedom they offered. I'd often take myself off to the park, especially during school holidays, when the fair would be on. I spent hours just watching all the different rides—dodgems were my favourite. I never went on any though, I was such a scaredy-cat!

Chapter 5

Move to the Red Rose County

Most Asian people who had settled in the north of England tended to work in the textile industry. This was the case for my father when we moved from Oxford to Bradford. He became a weaver in one of the many cotton mills that were still going strong in the late 1960s and early 1970s.

Unfortunately, the cotton industry was declining rapidly in Yorkshire, and in 1973, my father was made redundant when his mill closed. However, the cotton industry was still going strong in Lancashire, and he became a weaver at Moss Bridge, in Darwen, near Blackburn. Together with India Mill, again in Darwen, and Courtaulds, in Preston, it kept going for another decade or so.

Our first house in Blackburn was at 41 Quarry Street, near Larkhill Health Centre (now closed), a short distant from the town centre. This was a modest two-up two-down, with a kitchen in the back room and an outside toilet. My father later built a single-storey extension, adjoining the back room (without knowing he needed planning permission), and the kitchen was moved out there. This provided much-needed extra space in the back room. The house had some modern facilities, though. For example, there were gas fires, so we didn't have to lug coal from the cellar or suffer the discomfort of smoke in our eyes from getting the fire going. But the outside loo was a pain.

Looking back, I don't know how the six of us managed in a two-bedroomed mid-terraced house. It soon became apparent to my father that three young boys sharing one bedroom was becoming an issue, with Zaman sleeping on a bed/settee in the front room. Zaman was working in Courtaulds and giving all his wages to my father. With two wages coming in, it soon enabled my father to buy the adjoining property at number 43, into which Zaman, George, and Amjid moved, joining us at mealtimes.

At Moss Bridge my father was truly valued as an employee, as he had never taken a single day off sick or been late for work. That was his work ethic. Moss Bridge regarded him so highly they were happy for him to take six to eight weeks' holidays all at once and keep his job open when he returned. He would use the holidays to visit his family in Pakistan.

***

It was in Blackburn that the arguments between my parents really came to the fore and became more frequent. As I recall, they were often over my mother complaining about how much money my father was sending to his family in Pakistan. Strange really that she didn't mind my father sending money to the village elders—she believed that was his obligation—but she felt he should send less to his family and spend more on the things that were needed here.

At that age, I didn't understand their arguments, but they began to occupy my mind. I remember my father being very loud, as most Pakistani men were in those days, which used to frighten me. But he was never violent towards my mother.

Moving home also meant a new school for me—my final one. I spent two years in the sixth form at Witton Park Comprehensive School on Buncer Lane. By the time I started my second year, we'd bought the adjoining property, and I had a room of my own. My parents had hoped that a room of my own would give me the privacy needed to study more effectively; they still clung to their dream of me becoming a doctor.

If only this was the case. It didn't take long for me to fill my head with all sorts of negative thoughts. My parents' arguments should have given me the motivation to study harder and be more determined to make something of myself. Instead, it sent me in the opposite direction. I began to think there is no point in studying; it would never bring my parents together, and we'd never be happy. My routine, day after day, was to have my tea and then go to my room and waste hour upon hour playing card games, usually solitaire, before falling asleep. Being in my room allowed me to escape from everyone into another world, where I did not have to face anyone.

I left Belle Vue Boys Grammar with six CSEs, achieving grade 1 in maths, thanks to the efforts of my private tutor. At Witton Park, I struggled in every subject, including maths, and left with two O levels.

If only my parents knew I hadn't used my time to study. In a way, I wished they had found out; it may have forced me to face reality or at least buck up my ideas. I can't fully explain why I was like that, other than what I have already said. I know of many other Pakistani children whose parents went through difficult times and argued, but many of them were inspired by their circumstances and went on to attain greater academic success. Some of them went on to have successful careers in medicine and law. Either would have been a dream come true for my parents. What went wrong for me?

Unlike most children, who may have rebelled or got up to mischief, I simply went further into my shell. All those lonely hours spent in my room did nothing to improve my social skills or my shy personality, making conversations with people painfully difficult whilst eroding any sense of self-esteem. I struggled to see a way past my self-pity, taking every opportunity to escape to my daydreaming. I also turned more and more to my only other outlet, football.

It was at Witton Park that I managed to play for the school team. The school didn't have a team for the sixth form; however, our fifth formers had been banned for fighting, and the school was asked if they could still fulfil the remaining fixtures, playing them as 'friendlies'. Our sports master, a Mr Cameron, asked boys from the sixth form if they wanted to play, and most of us jumped at the chance.

Playing more and more football helped me escape from many of my perceived failures, as well as from my parents' arguments. At one point, I thought they were going to split up—after all they had gone through in Pakistan and just when they should be able to enjoy life. Maybe I was overthinking it, making it a much bigger issue than it was. No one from the Pakistani community ever split up in those days.

Again, it may seem as if I am blaming my educational failure on my parents. Not at all. In their own way, they tried to support me as much as possible—private tuition, my own room, and extra pocket money. All to no avail. A lot of it was down to me and the way I interpreted what was going on around me. I lacked focus, motivation, and a sense of direction. My head was usually in the clouds, still dreaming of becoming a footballer or meeting someone who would sweep me off my feet. I often thought about running away, but that's as far as it got; I lacked the courage to do anything.

I should have left school after my second year at Witton and gotten myself a job. But I was indecisive and terrified of telling my parents how badly I was doing at school. Instead, I made up another lie. I pretended to be at school. As far as the school was concerned, I had left; as far as my parents were concerned, I was still at school, studying for my A levels.

Each morning, I would leave home around eight thirty, returning home at approximately four thirty. My routine was always the same— each morning, I would buy a return ticket to Preston, Burnley, or Bolton, spending the day in shopping centres, in the library, or just wandering the streets. Luckily, as I was supposed to be sixth-former, I did not have to wear a uniform.

All the dreams I'd had as a boy in Pakistan, built up by all those around me telling me how I would go to England, study hard, and one day return as the village doctor, were as far removed from reality as were my dreams of playing for Manchester United.

I believed I had failed miserably and felt deeply ashamed of letting everyone down, especially my parents. And yet, I kept up my lies and pretence. Day after day, I hoped and prayed I wouldn't run into anyone I knew; I had prepared excuses, just in case. My parents were so trusting of me, and I only got away with it because of their trust and how little they knew about schooling in this country. This only added to my anguish.

Most, if not all, my early school reports described me as 'academically average' and noted how well behaved I was—never doing anything wrong, but never achieving anything either. When I think about my early life, I cannot help but see it as such a waste of opportunity.

While pretending to be at school one day, I saw an advert for a week-long computer course in London. I can't remember where I saw it, but it was something that really appealed to me. As my parents continued to give me more than enough pocket money, I started to save most of it, stuffing bank notes into the pages of my books. Without telling my parents, I sent off for the course and then told them the school had arranged a week-long trip to a London college, which ran courses on studying for a degree.

This was also the time I experienced my first ever train ride, after having been in this country for nearly ten years. To be perfectly honest, I can't remember anything about the train journey down to London, where I caught the train from, or where I got off.

I was extremely anxious about the course. What would I do afterwards? Would I continue to pretend to be at school and for how long? These questions were going round and round my head, making me more and more anxious about where I was going in life.

Once I got to London, the company delivering the course also arranged lodgings for me. I made my way to the lodgings; again, I can't remember exactly where they were or how I got there, but I think I stayed somewhere in Golders Green. I don't recall anything about the course, except that I spent most of my time in my room each evening, worrying about what to do once I got back to Blackburn. Worrying was all I did; I never thought of doing anything.

As it turned out, the course itself was only an introductory one, with quite basic input on computers. At the end of the week, we were told about a more extensive course, which was much longer. But besides the cost, how would I explain it to my parents?

I now believe that, if I had told my parents, they would have supported me despite their initial disappointment, especially if I was serious about a career in computers. I never found the courage, though. I was terrified of telling my parents the truth about school and equally terrified of being found out. I returned home, starting my pretence once again.

Before I leave my schooling days behind, I have a few more memories from Witton Park to share.

When I played football in Bradford, I had played as a goalkeeper although I'd always considered myself to be an outfield player. In Blackburn, especially at school, Mr Cameron, played me in the centre of defence—not because I was outstanding in the air, or robust in my tackles, but because I had pace. He recognised my ability to intercept, my passing ability, and my overall reading of the game, like Franz Beckenbauer. I wish!

I really believed that, if someone had taken me under their wing early enough, I had the ability to be a good ball-playing defender, something I went on to enjoy in the local leagues and later in the seven-a-side league at Lancashire Constabulary.

Mr Cameron encouraged me a great deal, which gave me some confidence, even if it was only on the football pitch.

My highlight at school was to play in the team that played an annual match against the teachers in 1975. I even have a photo as a memento of the match, which we won.

One of my worst memories at this school is being attacked by a group of school bullies during one lunchtime. But it wasn't a racist attack. The gang simply picked on everyone.

During one lunchtime, about a dozen of us were playing on the school fields, when a gang of about six descended upon us and decided to take our football. I didn't wait for anyone else to say or do anything. Acting on pure impulse, and probably driven by my passion for football, I charged at the boy who had our ball, knocked him to the ground, and took it back.

Big mistake!

I didn't even have time to feel pleased with myself; the whole gang 'jumped' me. All I remember is being on the ground and being kicked and punched from all sides. After what seemed an eternity, they stopped because one of the lads I was playing with ran off to find a teacher. Amazingly, I walked away with only my pride hurt and a few minor cuts and bruises.

Being physically attacked and beaten is painful. However, suffering physical pain is nothing compared with the mental torture I put myself through when I embarrassed myself in front of my fellow pupils in another incident.

I was in the school library, with nearly twenty other pupils, all revising for our mock exams.

You know, sometimes the harder you try to suppress or stop something, the harder it is to do that. This was one of those moments for me. Suddenly, I felt a fart developing. I tried my best to suppress it, but the harder I tried, the worse it got. It managed to escape and those around me heard it. I was mortified. Being vastly different back then, I honestly didn't think I would survive such an incident. That awful feeling stayed with me for weeks, during which time I expected something terrible to happen, even though none of the pupils said anything. In those days, breaking wind in public was not 'cool'; you felt hugely embarrassed if it happened to you. Today, however, for some children, it seems to be a badge of honour, something to boast about.

My next memory concerns a girl. I wonder what my sons, Mehboob and Bashir, think of their old man, reading about me and girls at school? Worse still, I wonder what my parents would have made of it. I think I know the answer to that one!

Anyway, this young lady was called Hazel (not her real name). She was much quieter than the girl I introduced you to at Frizinghall. Hazel was shy and generally kept herself to herself, which in itself was an attraction for me. However, as was the case with the first girl, I still had the same issue—the inability to take any kind of action or make a move towards girls.

The fear of my parents and of bringing dishonour and shame on them was not something I could overcome. On top of that, the thought of Hazel rejecting me was too much for me to bear. I spent two whole years at school pontificating about what I should do and left school having done nothing. I never came across Hazel after that, often wondering what I'd do if I saw her.

You're right—probably nothing!

Today, when I look back to my time at school, all I see is how fear crippled my thinking and quite literally shut me down, with my intense timidness impeding my growth and development—such a waste of opportunity.

Chapter 6

'A Prince Returning Home'

Ever since I left my village, I had shamefully thought little about my extended family or other people from my village. My mind was occupied by coming to terms with my new surroundings, coping at school, or worrying about whether I would ever meet my parents' expectations and dreams. The village I grew up in, the people I knew, and the children I'd played with had been pushed to the back of my mind as my anxiety and inability to deal with things started to take control.

'Going back home'—now there's a phrase that has caused much controversy and debate. What is 'home' for those who have come to live here from the Asian subcontinent, or indeed from other parts of the world? Like others who've settled in Britain, we Pakistanis often use this term when describing the countries that we, our parents, and our grandparents came from.

But do we still regard those countries as our homes? In my view, a sizeable proportion of first- and second-generation Pakistanis do, despite having settled in this country permanently. By contrast, many third- and fourth-generation Pakistanis also use this term when talking about those countries, but I believe they do not consider those countries as their 'home'. They may speak fondly of those countries, but for most of them, Britain is their home.

Speaking for myself, the country of my birth will always hold a special place in my heart; my early memories of the village and its people will always bring a smile to my face. However, no matter how special Pakistan is to me, where I now live, with its wonderful weather, is my home.

Back in 1975, when I was pretending to be at school, my father suggested that a visit to Pakistan would be appropriate. Even though my extended family had been pushed to the back of my mind, they had not forgotten me. In their letters, they constantly asked about me. In more recent letters, they'd been asking my father to send me back, as my grandmother's health was deteriorating. My father felt he could not turn down such a request, so it was decided I would visit my relatives, along with my cousin George.

I didn't know how to feel about it all. As with most things, I had outwardly developed a way about me that didn't give much away—just in case the messages I was giving off were wrong. I had learned to react to other people's behaviour in a way that was 'safe'. This is a behaviour that some people adopt when they're not sure how to react or behave when something is said or something happens, rather than being themselves. This had become my default for most of my childhood and young adult life, all somehow connected to my fear of getting things wrong.

When my father told me he was sending me to Pakistan, I began to think about all those I had left behind and secretly became excited at the prospect of seeing them again. Unfortunately, the negative thoughts were not too far away either, leaving me anxious with silly little worries and insecurities.

As it turned out, it was an unbelievable experience. The flight from Manchester to Islamabad went without any hiccups. We'd been warned about the officials at the airport in Islamabad and that a small tip would help us through customs.

As we cleared customs, we were immediately surrounded by at least ten of our relatives, our welcoming party. They'd hired a van and asked two family friends to bring their cars to the airport, so there would be enough room for everyone, as well as our luggage.

As soon as we left the airport building, and even though it was the middle of December, the stifling heat hit us straight away, and the sweat started pouring. The humidity got worse as we climbed into the waiting vehicles; even with the windows wide open, it did little to cool us down. It reminded me of the heat that used to burn the soles of my feet all those years ago; thankfully, I now had brand-new shoes on my feet.

The smiling faces of our greeting party took our minds off the heat. The sheer joy in their faces was so sincere and comforting, and the women in the party just couldn't stop hugging and kissing us. I had never experienced such open displays of emotion. I was totally overwhelmed. Any negative thoughts I had were forgotten by the wonderfully happy reaction we received.

There is such amazing and reassuring beauty in the smiling human face.

The journey from the airport took approximately three hours. It soon flew by though, especially as we were being bombarded with many questions by people whose faces and names I had forgotten.

***

Sadly, there was one thing that even this wonderful reception could not hide. As soon as we left the airport area, it all came flooding back—the level of poverty I had almost erased from my memory. As we drove along the main road, I could not believe the condition of the houses we saw. We're not talking about rural villages; this was in the middle of the capital of Pakistan. The houses reminded me of the photos I'd seen of the townships of Soweto, South Africa. The only difference here was that these houses were not made from metal sheets but from mud, which put them at risk of being swept away by heavy rains. Yet, next to these mud houses were what I can only describe as little palaces. The contrast between the 'haves' and the 'have-nots' was stark. Worse was to follow.

I was shocked by the appearance of most of the people going about their daily business. They wore dirty and tattered old clothes; many were still barefoot. Some looked like walking skeletons, so thin you could count their ribs. I was amazed they had the strength to walk.

It seemed to me that the ten years I had been away had made little difference to the lives of these people. From what I'd seen so far, there had not been the kind of progress those village elders had hoped for when they'd first sent my father to England.

***

If the welcome we received at the airport was great, the welcome laid on for us when we got to our village was simply out of this world—totally unexpected and something I have never witnessed before or since. It seemed as if the whole village had turned out, and it quite literally took my breath away. There were people there we barely recognised, some I had completely forgotten, so many I didn't know. Some of those who'd come to see us had walked miles from nearby villages; when news of our arrival reached them, they all wanted to see the son of 'Lala Malik', as they referred to my father.

They were all lined up along the main street, all the way from the outskirts of our village to our house. There were flowers, banners, flags, and multicoloured confetti all around. It truly was a spectacle to behold. The scene was more befitting a wedding than two boys on a visit from England.

What on earth had we, had I, done to deserve such a welcome? I asked myself. Of course, it had nothing to do with me, but everything to do with my father and how highly he was regarded by those people. How they felt about my father, the way they all turned out to see his son come 'home' truly made me feel like a prince.

All I had known was failure, all I had felt was insecurity, and yet here I was in the middle of all these people so happy to see me. It was a remarkably humbling and emotional feeling.

Perhaps describing my father's popularity in this way may seem over the top, but that's exactly how he was regarded, not just by our village but also by the surrounding villages. I do not think my words can ever do him justice. He was an incredibly considerate man and went to great lengths to try to help others in any way he could; that is why so many held him in such high regard.

The sad thing about it is that I will always feel as if I've let him and all those people down. No matter what I achieve in life, it will never compensate for the fact that I have shattered so many dreams.

As we got out of the van and walked towards our family home, occupied by my grandmother, my two uncles and their wives, and my uncle Rakhman's three children, people started throwing flowers in front of us. Some relatives greeted us with flower garlands, throwing them around our necks. Both George and I looked at each other in bewilderment and delight; neither of us knew how to react, so we just smiled and lapped it all up.

It was the most genuinely happiest feeling I had experienced up to then. The greetings and celebrations went on well into the early hours of the morning, and we got little sleep that night. Our adrenaline carried us through the next few days.

Those next few days were a constant stream of visitors, who expected a present, a letter, or some news of their loved ones in England. It didn't matter what the present was, how big or small, or it's cost—the fact that it had come all the way from England made their day. The presents included items of clothing, watches, pens, shoes, and toys. And for some, there was a personal letter, which meant just as much.

Naturally, with all these presents and gifts, we'd been well over our baggage allowance and had to pay for the extra weight—not that this mattered to my father. To him, the joy the gifts brought to those people was worth it.

***

After a few days, once the visitors had slowed down and I'd recovered from the infamous 'Delhi belly', I decided to visit my Uncle Ghani, my mother's eldest brother. I knew that, of all her family, he was the one she was closest to, and she wanted me to see him. Uncle Ghani was in the army; he was stationed in Bahawalpur, about a day's ride on the train southeast from Jhelum. As luck would have it, I was joined on this journey by my cousin Akhtar, my Aunt Muzambil's eldest son who, coincidently, was also in Pakistan and jumped at the chance to visit our uncle.

On our journey to Bahawalpur, Akhtar was a great companion. His extrovert personality was just what I needed to help me along. We spent three days with my uncle in his private quarters. He'd be at work during the day (not sure what he did exactly, as he never spoke about it), and he took us out for meals and walks around Bahawalpur in the evenings.

Bahawalpur was vastly different from my village, with solid buildings, though many were owned by the army. The roads had pavements, and the climate there was also cooler, helping to make it a pleasant stay.

***

Akhtar and I had always got on well. He was a couple of years younger than me, but he was much more attuned to life. Like his mother, Akhtar never shied away from standing up for what was right, never ran from a fight or worried about speaking his mind. Strong, good-looking, and athletic, he also had a rebellious streak. Akhtar would have been the ideal son for my father.

Of all my cousins and children of my extended family, Akhtar clearly stood out. He excelled at most sports and won many prizes at school. He was also the one who seemed to have a smile on his face most of the time, a quality he inherited from his mother. He had this look in his eyes that told you he was either going to get up to something, or he'd already done something that was going to get him into trouble. I admired him greatly and secretly wanted to be like him. Out of all the children within my extended family, he'd have been the one to have the courage to have a mixed-race relationship, but he settled down, happily, in an arranged marriage.

Unfortunately, in later life, Akhtar developed several illnesses, including kidney failure, diabetes, and cataracts, ultimately suffering a series of strokes that left him paralyzed and bed bound. Despite this, Akhtar also had his mother's courage and her fighting spirit, and he fought until the bitter end. Akhtar sadly lost this battle and passed away in early 2015. He will be sorely missed by all those who knew him.

Just like his mother, Akhtar was taken from us far too soon. If ever there were two people deserving of heaven, they were it.

May the Almighty grant them both Jannat.

***

Travelling around in Pakistan was, and still is, quite chaotic. The trains and buses are always jam-packed, with every inch of space taken by passengers or animals. Apart from the main GT Road, which was tarmacked, most roads were nothing more than dirt tracks; even the GT Road had huge potholes. There were no streetlights back then, no road markings, and no such thing as a right of way. In fact, there was no give way at all. The road space was equally fought over by humans, motor vehicles, and animals. You would literally be taking your life into your hands every time you crossed the road.

Although there was a lot less vehicle traffic in our village, it was still busy with people and animals. However, the chaos I found around me only seemed to bother me, while George and Akhtar seemed to take it in their stride.

On more recent visits, not only did I find the incredibly busy roads difficult to deal with, but there was also the risk of being robbed at gunpoint or being kidnapped. There were organised gangs who targeted people from abroad, as they knew those returning would bring back money and other valuables. We were warned to steer well clear of certain areas and roads that were notorious for violent robberies.

George and I stayed in Pakistan for approximately three weeks, rounding our visit off with several meals laid on by family members, some of my father's friends, and the village elders.

Chapter 7

My First Job

Upon my return to England, I once again began my nightmare pretence of going to school all over again. However, following a further six months of hell, my fortunes took a turn for the better.

A Pakistani bank, by the name of United Bank Limited (UBL), had started to expand in the United Kingdom. They already had branches in several towns and cities with large Pakistani populations and were looking to open a branch in Blackburn that year.

My old friend Hamid, from Bradford—the Chelsea fan—had joined this bank straight from school. He had no problem getting the job and quickly became popular with his colleagues. We'd kept in touch with regular visits. During one of those visits, he told me about an opportunity with the bank in Blackburn. Knowing my predicament, he asked if I would be interested. I told him I didn't dare tell my parents about school. He said, 'How long are you going to keep that up?' He finally managed to persuade me to apply and encouraged me to tell my parents about the bank.

To my utter surprise and delight, my parents saw working in a bank as a prestigious and respectable profession. When I told them about an opportunity with UBL, they agreed for me to leave school and apply for a position. I knew they were both extremely disappointed with me not going to university, but they hid it well.

And so, with a great deal of support from Hamid, I obtained my first job in 1976, as a cashier/clerk with UBL. I was almost twenty years old. I should have been excited, but I was utterly nervous about it all.

UBL was a Pakistani government-owned bank; its recruitment process, and the way it was run, were completely different from the way banks operate in this country. When I applied for my position, it was not a case of meeting the required qualifications, getting through the application form, an in tray exercise, or an interview. Oh no, nothing like that. To meet the UBL's criteria, I had to demonstrate—or rather my father had to demonstrate—how well known he was within the Pakistani community in Blackburn and surrounding areas and how much influence he had over them. From the UBL's perspective, the more people he knew, the more potential clients he was able to bring to the bank. My father had to provide names of all the Pakistani families he knew and could confidently expect to open accounts with the bank. Luckily for me, he was very well known.

Throughout the process, there were no questions for me to answer. I just had to sit there and smile, while my father answered them all.

At the time, the bank mainly wanted clients to open deposit accounts; it offered no mortgages, whilst current accounts were offered to well-established businesses. The biggest source of income for the bank came from clients who regularly sent money back to their families in Pakistan. Once the branch became more established, it started to provide more mainstream banking facilities, such as secured loans and current accounts, with mortgages following later.

Having got my first job under my belt, the thoughts of lying to my parents about school and my lack of academic achievements were slowly and mercifully drifting away. During my probationary period, I was shown how to open deposit accounts. Once I'd mastered the process, I spent most of my first three months on the road. With my father beside me, I visited as many potential clients as I could, trying to persuade them to open accounts. I had moderate success doing this; more people agreed to open accounts when my father was with me than when I was on my own. Despite my introverted personality, I managed to get through my probationary period.

I was overjoyed with my first ever wage packet of around sixty pounds. I had promised my first wage to my mother. She promptly sent it to her brother in Pakistan for him to divide equally among the poor and the homeless. She had always told me that my first earnings should be given away to those whose needs were greater than ours, and if I did that, then Allah Tallah would always smile on me.

Every subsequent pay packet went to my father as head of the family. I only kept ten pounds each week for my pocket money. This was the norm in Pakistani households.

Although I felt I'd landed on my feet with this job, my own shortcomings soon caught up with me. By the time I'd completed my first six months, my lack of people skills and my inability to hold conversations or build any kind of rapport with existing or potential clients were becoming very apparent to the bank manager, newly arrived from Pakistan. But he was quite patient with me. He could see how nervous I was and did his best to put me at ease. Unfortunately, shortly after I'd completed my probationary period, he was transferred to a bigger branch in the Midlands.

My new manager and I never hit it off at all. In fact, I detested him, and I began to hate my job. I'd now landed myself in another dilemma; how was I going to get myself out of this one?

Most people, when they have a problem, either seek help and advice or are creative enough to find a solution themselves. Back then, I tended to worry, bury my head in the sand, and hope things would get better. Whenever my parents asked, I pretended to be happy in my job; this went on for another two years.

Eventually, the worry and anxiety led me to have crippling stomach pains, like the ones I'd suffered in Pakistan as a child. I had no choice but to seek medical help from my GP. He suspected an ulcer and sent me for tests at the hospital; thankfully, they came back negative. When my GP found out about my work situation, he advised me to leave work; otherwise, I could develop ulcers. He also persuaded me to let him speak to my parents and explain what could happen if my situation continued. Reluctantly, and with the pains getting worse, I agreed.

Again, to my amazement, my parents told me to leave my job straight away. If I hadn't been so fearful of my parents, I would have seen how understanding they really were. My first working experience was, without doubt, my worst, and I saw it as another failure.

***

Sorry, you're fired!

Another sad memory from that job concerns the lady who worked there as a cleaner. She was married and often brought her young daughter with her. Hard-working and conscientious, she was never late, always doing more than she was required to do and often staying well beyond her two hours. Nothing was too much trouble for her; she only spoke to ask if we wanted anything else doing.

For some reason, the new manager didn't like her and wanted to get rid of her. Yet he didn't have the bottle to do his dirty deed himself, so he asked me to sack her instead. Sack someone? Me? I couldn't even say something nice to anyone, let alone fire them!

Of course, I found the task difficult and dealt with it in my own feeble and stuttering way. I made up a lie, telling her we were no longer able to afford a cleaner. Even now I cringe at what I did to that poor lady and the memory of how she looked up at me with her sad eyes. She accepted it with such dignity. I am appalled at what I did.

Chapter 8

My Footballing Years: The Local Asian Football Scene

Admittedly, reading about a game played by twenty-two players chasing after and kicking a leather ball, full of wind, may not capture everyone's imagination. But that's not how we lovers of the beautiful game see it; for us, it is much, much more than that.

This chapter is about the immense impact football has had on a boy who could not have foreseen this very English game. It's about my footballing idols, about my dreams and aspirations of making it big and playing for my beloved Manchester United.

This chapter goes on to provide some insight into the Asian youngsters playing football locally, the challenges they faced, and how they overcame some of them.

***

Mahmood Ahmed

Every football fan around at the time went through the magical euphoria of what happened in summer 1966.

Except me.

I had moved to England only a few months earlier; however, England winning our first and only World Cup completely escaped me. Like most Asians who had recently made England their home, I'd never heard of football. I don't even remember football being part of any PE lessons at either of my first schools, in Oxford or Bradford. I don't recall anyone talking about it, which must be a memory lapse, as I'm sure they would have talked about nothing else. I know my family and friends never talked about it; they had no interest in it. It must have been in the papers and on the TV, but I never read the papers, and we didn't have a television set until after the World Cup, so I missed out on England's biggest footballing achievement.

As I recall, football was something I discovered quite by chance, in Bradford. It had a different meaning for a while, with my embarrassing thoughts about why a certain Mr Busby came to teach at Belle Vue Boys' Grammar and my imagination completely running away with how he was going to help me play for my beloved United.

One evening after school, I was (genuinely) walking to the library when I saw some boys playing on a piece of dirt ground opposite Drummond School in Bradford, a few hundred yards from where I lived. I stopped along the school wall to watch them kicking and, more strangely, heading a large round ball. I remember thinking to myself how weird and funny they looked. I was about to walk on when one of them beckoned me over and asked if I wanted to join in. Straight away, I said no, telling him I'd never played this game and didn't know how to. By now the other boys had also stopped playing and came over. They all started encouraging me to join in. Reluctantly, and feeling totally embarrassed and unsure, I agreed, as felt I pressurised.

I wish I could tell you I was a natural at this newfound game, but compared with the other boys, my first attempts at kicking the ball were quite comical. All the things they could do easily and without effort, I struggled with. Several times, I missed kicking the ball completely, even falling over a few times when trying to kick it. Some of the boys laughed at my pathetic attempts. Embarrassed and wanting to avoid making a bigger fool of myself, I was about to storm off when the boy who first spoke to me got hold of my arm and said, 'Don't let them put you off. We were all like that at first. We've been playing for a long time now.'

Zak, I later discovered, also happened to be a United fan, from Yorkshire of all places!

From that moment on, and after many, many attempts at kicking the ball, I was hooked. Football was all I could think about. I played at every opportunity. Soon, running around after the ball, tackling, heading, and sweating bucketloads seemed to help me forget all my worries. Football took me to another place, another world—a world where only playing football mattered. Soon Hamid and I started to play regularly on the school concrete ground.

Whether I was playing on the school playground or some rough dirt ground, football allowed me to be me. No thoughts of studying or school, no thoughts of what I couldn't do, no worrying about what was happening with my parents or how far I was from ever fulfilling their dreams. It didn't even worry me how bad I was at football. I just wanted to play whenever I could.

I soon picked up the basics and absolutely loved the way it made me feel. To run with the ball, beat defenders, and score was exhilarating. I couldn't get enough of it. Football took me to a place where I was not this timid and extremely shy boy but, rather, an equal.

The sad thing was that, while my parents didn't directly tell me not to play football, they never mentioned football or any other sport when they talked about their aspirations for me. For their generation, it was imperative that children spend their valuable time studying, not wasting time on silly games the English played. I would hear them say, 'We are here to work or to study, so that we can go back to our homelands as soon as possible, to show what we have achieved during our time here.' Such talk frightened me, and I convinced myself that, if I wanted to play football, it would be behind their backs.

Perhaps you've had similar experiences of wanting to do something different from what your parents had in store for you, and you too found it difficult to go against their wishes. That certainly was the case for me.

Whilst playing on the concrete at Drummond School, someone a few years older than us joined in. He was called Rubani. He was much better at football than any of us, and it was no surprise to learn that he played regularly for Wilsden, a village not far from Bradford. Rubani could tell that we were all very keen, but there was no one to organise us, so he took it upon himself to do that. He started by providing some structure for us, organising regular training sessions two or three times a week after school and at the weekends. These became my regular visits to the 'library' as far as my parents were concerned.

Within a few months of rigorous training, Rubani felt the only way we were going to get better was to play regular matches against other teams. He entered us into the Yorkshire Red Triangle Under-16 League.

Rubani was the first Asian man I came across who played football. I say man. I mean a young adult; he was in his late teens or early twenties. Rubani was a very decent defender, muscular and athletic, with blistering pace. He was also extremely competitive. Furthermore, he had great leadership qualities, and we all looked up to him. I guess, he was what you might call our first role model. He was so different to all the other Pakistani men we knew. He spoke to us in English and told jokes. We found it easy to relate to him. He spoke to us as if we were of similar age; he was patient with those of us who struggled to express ourselves, especially quiet ones like me; and he respected our views, even if he did not agree with them. We all liked him. He was like our elder brother.

It was his respect for other people's views that struck a chord with me, even though I didn't realise it then, and it was this that influenced me hugely later in life.

Rubani pulled us all together and let us choose a name for our team, Carlisle United, and registered us with the league. We didn't choose this name because we supported the then Division Two team from Cumbria; in fact, we'd never heard of them. It was chosen because we all lived close to Carlisle Street, just up the road from Drummond School. We used whatever pocket money we had and paid for the team kit, a couple of footballs and a pump. Rubani made up any shortfalls. I saved like mad to buy a pair of football boots.

At the time, there were no other Asian teams in that league, none that we were aware of. It was still a rarity to come across a team with a Pakistani player in their side, let alone a team made up of all Pakistani players. We felt very proud of being the first all-Pakistani team to play in that league.

What position did I play? Well as you will have gathered by now, I hadn't been great at pushing myself forward or making decisions, so I was pushed into being the team goalie. I'd never played in that position but accepted the decision without too much dissent; besides, nobody else volunteered.

I lacked many of the goalie's attributes. I wasn't very tall or powerfully built; wasn't all that athletic; and, certainly in the beginning, I was not particularly good at diving to make saves like the great Gordon Banks or Peter 'the Cat' Bonetti. I did have good reflexes though, and that was good enough for the team at the time.

Apart from the pride we felt, the only real memory I have of that league was that we handsomely beat most if not all the teams in our division. Sadly, and shamefully, after some of these games, we were often attacked and assaulted by opposing players and their parents. This could have been because they were just bad losers, but the language they used left us in no doubt. They did not like being beaten by a bunch of 'Pakis'. I guess they found it hard to stomach the fact that we could beat an all-white team whose ancestors had invented the game. The truth of the matter is that racism didn't just exist within the minds of a few 'skinheads'; it also came out on a football pitch, where the so-called decent children and their parents couldn't stomach being beaten by those whose skin colour was different.

When you're a victim of such attacks, it can be difficult not to stereotype and label everyone from the white community as racist. I didn't understand why people behaved in such a way back then. But years later, through the job I did—and my early experiences helped—I came to better understand what can cause this behaviour. The environment we grow up in, the behaviour of those around us, and our circumstances all help shape our thoughts of those who are 'different' and can lead some of us to blame, to hurl verbal abuse, or to attack them.

It was in Bradford, through meeting Zak, that I fell in love with Manchester United. Naturally, Zak was a big influence on who I supported. All he could talk about was Bobby Charlton, Dennis Law, and Georgie Best. I wanted to learn more about them, and it inspired me to make proper use of the library and read up about them and the legendary Sir Matt Busby. I read voraciously about the Munich air disaster; Sir Matt and Bobby's fight for survival; and the heroics of United's goalkeeper, Harry Gregg. If there was one subject that captivated me and drew me to reading, it was football and Manchester United. Sir Matt and Sir Bobby's struggles to overcome their life-threatening injuries to manage and play for the team drew me to United like a bee to a honeypot.

But living in Yorkshire, I naturally got a lot of stick for supporting United. Stubbornly, the more stick I got, the more entrenched my support for United became.

***

After we moved to Blackburn, I managed to find the courage to tell my parents I was playing football. And to my great relief, they accepted it. By seventeen, I was playing for the school team and with older boys and young men, all Asians, on some grassy land besides St Albans church, near Quarry Street.

I've mentioned how we all suffered racism at school and while playing football. Now I faced it again but from the unlikeliest of places—from other Asians. There was me thinking it was only something white people did!

All those who played on the grassy patch next to St Alban's Church were British Indians. When I first saw them playing there, I just sat down and watched them and waited until they finished before approaching them.

I'd waited for well over an hour when they finally sat down on the slopes for a rest. I introduced myself. I told them I was very keen to play and asked if I could turn up next weekend. The first question they asked me was, 'Are you Pakistani?' When I said I was, they immediately told me not to bother, as they didn't allow Pakistanis to play with them.

I couldn't believe what I was hearing! These guys were not white; they were brown like me. Thankfully, this was my first and only experience of racism from my fellow Asians. Unfortunately, when we start to negatively label those who are different from us, it isn't difficult to discriminate against them in some way. Unless we are prepared to interact and keep an open mind and willing to learn about others, we are all capable of discrimination without seeing it as such. My experience with Shantilal had proved that. These days, I believe they call this 'unconscious bias'.

However, my passion for football was not going to let something like that get in the way. For several weeks, I continued to turn up each weekend, at the same time, pleading with them to let me play. Week after week, I got the same response. After several more weeks, they did offer an explanation. They said they were worried I would start fighting; according to them, that was what all Pakistanis did. I made every promise I could, but to no avail.

A few more weeks went by before they eventually relented and agreed to let me play—but only after I'd agreed to pay twice as much as everyone else (a pound, instead of fifty pence). The money didn't matter to me; I just wanted to play football.

The strange thing is, within a week after allowing me to play with them, they not only reduced my subs to the same as everyone else but also elected me as their captain. They very quickly realised I was no fighter, and in a strange way, I was quite proud to be their captain.

I know—captain of a team of lads having a kick about pales into insignificance compared to leading out my beloved United at Old Trafford. However, overcoming how those lads viewed me and the fact that, within a short period of time, their view about me changed so dramatically gave me a real sense of achievement, such a rare feeling for me.

Not playing as a goalkeeper, I now had the freedom to enjoy my football as an outfield player, a licence to run with the ball. I never knew how much skill and pace I had, compared to the other lads, that is. Admittedly, I was not particularly good in the air, but I usually played with someone who was 'an old-fashioned centre-half', who won all the headers and made the robust tackles. I intercepted, picked up the loose ball, and sprayed passes out of defence—a position I had made my own in the school team.

As someone who struggled in many areas of life, I found football much more than just kicking a leather ball around. It was my one and true form of escapism. Whether I was just having a kick about with one or two friends or playing a competitive match, for those moments, football took me away from all my insecurities, fears, failures, and worries.

Playing football was something I was good at, compared to those I was playing with. Even before I got to the playground, I started to imagine and dream of what I could achieve in football. And when I started playing, I felt I was in that dream wonderland. It was a place where I could dream about my heroes—the Laws; the Bests; and, above all, Sir Bobby. In that world, I could freely imagine I was playing with the young Bobby Charlton. Both Dennis Law and George Best were much more flamboyant, but Sir Bobby was the one I could really relate to. His background, his personality, and his fight for life after the Munich air crash were the same as what I believed I was like and what I was going through. They were all the things that, in my mind, helped me to bond so easily with my idol. I felt I was going through similar difficulties and traumas.

The reality, of course, was somewhat different. But in Sir Bobby's humble beginnings, I found an extraordinarily strong connection. Besides all that, he had always been such a gentleman, dealing with life in a dignified and respectful way—qualities I had always admired and aspired to.

But oh, how I would imagine every day being on that pitch at the theatre of dreams with my idol. I would be the one to square the ball to him for his famous body swerve and for him to smash the ball with one of his thunderbolts into the top corner at the Stretford end.

Can you, just for a moment, imagine it? Close your eyes and let the sound of Radio 5 Live from Old Trafford fill your ears:

> *Ahmed, the most unlikely of footballers—skinny, gangly-looking—picks up the ball outside his penalty area, runs through the Liverpool midfield. So silky smooth, cutting through their midfield like knife through butter.*

Why Liverpool? I hear you ask. Well, they have always been our greatest rivals.

> *He reaches the penalty area and sees the run of Charlton to his left. He squares the ball to the oncoming Charlton,*

who, without breaking stride, hits the ball first time, a glorious left footer. The ball flies into the back of the net, one-nil United. What a deadly duo they make, the unknown Ahmed and the legendary Charlton! This new kid is a perfect foil for the England international.

If only, if only!

***

Often when I went to play football at the weekends, Liaqat and Amjid would come along too. Liaqat always fancied himself as a bit of a football dribbler. He would try and go on many mazy runs, often choosing not to pass to his teammates. In frustration one of them shouted at him, 'Pass the bloody ball, Liaqat. Who do you think you are, George Best?' From that moment on, he was always known as George.

It was on that spare piece of land, playing with the other Indian lads a million miles from Old Trafford, where I met my second lifelong friend, Mohammed Aziz Osman, or 'Ossy' as he is known. My friendship with Ossy began with us falling out and almost squaring up to each other. Yes, I know, a timid boy like me getting into fights sounds unlikely, but it was true.

For several months, I'd been playing football with my new Indian friends and always dreamed of playing in United's red-and-white shirt. After saving furiously to buy it, I proudly wore it at the very next game.

As always, we picked two sides and started playing; Ossy was on the opposing side. I picked up the ball from the goalie and ran at the opposing players, reaching the opposition penalty area. As I went past Ossy, instinctively he tried to grab me and caught my shirt around the collar, ripping it slightly.

For some unexplained reason, the ripped shirt turned me into a 'red devil', screaming at Ossy. He was one of the most aggressive tacklers I'd ever played with or against; his bone-crunching tackles often left many players black and blue. He was also brilliant in the air with a powerful shot—rare for a defender.

However, Ossy was also a very passive young man. He just turned to me, and said, 'Sorry, mate. Don't worry. I'll get it mended for you.'

I just looked at him, gasped and then just burst out laughing. From that moment on, we became inseparable. The fact that he also happened to support United helped no end.

Ossy was the eldest of five children who had come over from East Africa in the early 1970s. He'd taken over from his father as the head of the family after his father sadly passed away. Ossy hadn't even reached his teens, and the family had only been in England a short time. There was so much expected of Ossy, and the pressure of expectation weighed heavily on his young shoulders.

Indian-Pakistani friendships were quite rare in those days, yet we became close, mainly because of all things football and United. It goes to show, given the chance, sport really can bring people together.

After school, when we were not playing football, I would be round to his house, playing carrom board. This was a game played on a wooden board approximately three feet square with holes at each corner. There were twenty-four wooden pieces, like drafts—twelve white and twelve black, a red one known as the queen and slightly larger plastic striker. The aim of the game was to use the striker to put all your pieces into the holes or pockets, and then the queen, before your opponent.

At the weekends. we'd be kicking the football about, training, and playing football tennis, just the two us, all day long. Even when we'd played a match, we would continue for hours on our own.

Like Hamid, my first friend, Ossy was much more focused than me, and he knew what he wanted after leaving school. He became an apprentice at the Royal Ordnance Factory (ROF) in Lower Darwen, near Blackburn. He now works as a property inspector for a housing association.

***

We were now in the late 1970s and early 1980s, and there was still no sign of any Asian footballers breaking into professional football.

There are, in my view several reasons for this, including:

1. There was a huge difference in the cultural psyche of Asians compared with white Europeans and black communities living in the United Kingdom. Asians, when it came to most sports— excluding cricket and hockey, as they were well established in the Indian subcontinent—were not huge participants. Many first-generation Asians considered their stay in this country as temporary, and sport was not part of their psyche. They regarded leisure activities as a distraction they could ill afford. Their thinking also influenced a lot of their children and grandchildren. It's a well-known fact that, for children to be successful in sport, they need encouragement, commitment, and huge support from their parents from an early age. As education was the main priority for many Asian parents, it was difficult for them to provide this vital support.

2. By the time most of the second generation's interest in football reached any significance, it was too late—the second- and third-generation children were too old. Just go down to any local park and watch a game, and you'll see how young children start. The coaching, training and advice on diet and nutrition all starts early if you are serious about giving your children a chance to be successful in sport; many Asians of my parents' generation had no idea about any of these things. The right kind of advice and support at the earliest opportunity is still largely missing, and it has taken too long for these attitudes to change.

3. Sadly, we are still unable to rid racism from our society, and this remains a barrier for Asian footballers trying to break into the game.

Let me provide you with an example for my first reason. Whilst working in my first job at the Pakistani bank, UBL, several of us got together to form an all-Asian team, Blackburn Dynamos, which played in an all-Asian league. In this team. there was one player, Manzur 'Manny' Khan who, when it came to strength, agility, skill, raw talent, and desire stood head and shoulders above us all. In his younger days, Manny had played for his school team and was given a trial by Blackburn Rovers. Whilst playing in a trial game for Rovers, he was secretly watched by a scout from Everton. After the game, the scout approached him and his father and tried to persuade them to come to trials with his club. The scout told them he was convinced the club would offer him a contract on schoolboy terms because Manny had what it took to become a professional footballer.

Unfortunately, his father flatly refused the opportunity for several reasons, distance being one; he also didn't consider football a serious profession, and he wanted his son to concentrate on his studies. Manny never got the chance to reach his potential or fulfil his dream of becoming a professional footballer.

Moving on to the issue of racism, it was highlighted in England's qualifying matches for Euro 2020 finals. Several of England's black players were victims of racist abuse, with a number speaking out publicly. There is no doubt that racism is still prevalent in our society. Several black players have cited racism at the highest level as the main reason for the lack of black managers in our game. Those still not convinced about the level of racism within football should read ex-Liverpool player John Barnes's story, along with others who describe how racism has impacted their careers.

However, I still believe, with the right approach, the hurdle of racism can be overcome. It has been proven by many men and women of colour who have succeeded in sport and other areas of life. It requires strength of character, commitment, and sheer determination to overcome the challenges of inequality; not all of us are blessed with such qualities.

It is a profound pity that a momentous hurdle must be faced by those with a different skin colour.

***

Going back to the local Asian scene, let me provide you with further insight of what it was like in the late seventies and early eighties by sharing the story of Blackburn Dynamos. In Blackburn, many Asians played grassroot football. Some played by getting together with friends and family members; these were not organised weekly matches but more like weekly kick abouts on a spare bit of grass or playground.

Like I did with those Indian lads at St Alban's, most played games at their local fields every weekend . After a while, this progressed into matches with other Asian teams within the Blackburn area as players became more competitive. It slowly led to some teams playing each other on a regular basis. This, in turn, led to several teams organising themselves better and forming an all-Asian league, though some players still joined mainstream leagues and played for predominantly white teams. Among the Asian teams was the team I played for, Blackburn Dynamos. The league had no name, but teams from Blackburn, Bolton, and Preston joined.

Blackburn Dynamos was the brainchild of Manny Khan. He brought several of us, playing for different teams, together at Blackburn Dynamos. He invited people like Faruk Dalal 'Faz', Mohammed Anayat 'Lato', Ossy, and me to a meeting in Lato's front room to discuss his vision and to come up with a name for the team. After settling on Blackburn Dynamos, we set about cherry-picking players from other teams to put together some of the best Asian players in Blackburn. From the group that played on St Alban's, Only Ossy and I were considered good enough for this new team, and the team was formed in 1978. Manny was elected the team captain and took it upon himself to organise training sessions and get us into shape.

There was one other player who later played a hugely supportive role in my working life, Ibrahim Master, or Ibby, as we all called him. Ibby and I went to Witton Park and played for the school team together. He was a tireless midfielder who never stopped running and who had the canny knack of scoring important goals at vital moments.

As with all teams, there were several additions and changes to the team over the following years, but the five of us remained the backbone of the team. My memory is particularly strong about one new player, Majid (not his real name), not purely for his footballing ability, but because he was the first Pakistani man, I knew who had a white girlfriend, later marrying her. It must have been incredibly difficult for them to go against their family, friends, and the wider community.

For Dynamos, I played in several positions—in goal; in midfield; and, on rare occasions, in attack too. However, it was in defence where Ossy and I formed a formidable central defensive partnership. Ossy was the dominant typical British centre half, while I was his sidekick. I dealt with the loose balls, made the short passes to our midfielders, or hit the long ones over the top for our strikers to chase. Ossy's reputation as a defender continued to grow. Eventually he went on to play for several white teams in the Saturday and Sunday leagues.

In our first and only season, we were unbeaten and running away with the league. But as was often the case with us Asians, if things didn't go our way, we lacked the discipline to work out our issues. We started to argue, resulting in the league being scrapped all together.

Blackburn Dynamos carried on playing friendly matches with other teams and later played in the seven-a-side league at Witton Park, Blackburn.

***

In 1981, during one friendly match, at Pleasington, I was playing in goals. I came rushing out of my penalty area for a fifty-fifty ball. Both the opposing forward and I missed the ball, but as our legs tangled, we crumpled to the ground. This innocuous collision resulted in my one and only serious injury. I broke my right leg, dislocated my right ankle, and tore ligaments and tendons in both ankles.

I remember the ambulance taking me to Blackburn Royal Infirmary, where I was left for hours on a trolley in the corridor, waiting to be seen. Eventually I had some stitches inserted in my right shin and my leg put in plaster.

For my parents, this injury was what they had feared all their lives. When I got home, they were shocked to see me on crutches. But again, they were immensely supportive. Looking back, it seems my fears about them were mainly in my head, as they provided support at several crucial moments in my life. I wish I could have seen how supportive they had always been at the time.

Before I bring this chapter to an end, I must share my final memory from my footballing days with Manny and the gang.

***

I had never been to a nightclub. This was not so unusual for Muslims in those days; largely for cultural and religious reasons, very few frequented nightclubs.

Anyway, following one friendly game, Manny and some of the others wanted to do something different, rather than go home or just go for a bite to eat. Manny, who always had a twinkle in his eye, suggested going for a night out, somewhere we had never been before, perhaps to a nightclub. At first, we all laughed. We told him we pushed the boat out just going for a curry. A nightclub? Was he crazy? What would happen if someone saw us? What would our parents think? Thanks, but no thanks we all said.

But Manny was undeterred; when he wanted to do something, he did it, even if he had to face the consequences later. He found a way to persuade us.

He suggested going for a curry and then to a nightclub in Manchester. That seemed to convince us; it was far enough away, and the chances of anyone seeing us there were practically nil.

The nightclub was called Pips; it has long since gone but was well known in those days. It was often advertised on the TV, and I still remember parts of the slogan. I think it went something like this: 'Come to the Pips, with its eleven dance floors. Pips, behind the cathedral.' In the end, five of us went. We took Manny's car, as he was the only one who drove. I remember there were five of us, as I had to grab five ties. You couldn't get in without a tie and shirt; it was part of the strict dress code.

It was not a great night for me. I was far too self-conscious, knowing I couldn't dance. I couldn't stop thinking everyone was looking at me. I was totally out of my comfort zone. I couldn't strike up a conversation—not that you could hear anything in all that din. But that didn't bother the others; I was surprised and rather envious to see them so at ease. I couldn't wait to get out of the place. Eventually, following what seemed an eternity, we decided to leave at around two o'clock, much to my relief.

As we were leaving, I seemed to perk up; suddenly and out of the blue, I had an idea. I'd never been to Old Trafford, to watch my beloved United. I hadn't even seen the ground. So quick as a flash, I said, 'Let's go to Old Trafford before we go home.'

You should have seen the looks on their faces—they were gobsmacked!

'Are you mad?' one of them said. 'It's two o'clock in the morning! The place is shut. You won't be able to see a thing.'

'I know,' I pleaded, 'but at least I'll be able to say I've seen Old

Trafford, even if only from the outside. I probably won't get another opportunity. I'd like to go, please.'

Luckily, most were United fans, so they relented.

And so, we went to see the theatre of my dreams. None of them could have known how much this special ground meant to me. Some of the greatest, if not the greatest players ever to grace the British game, had fulfilled their dreams there. Part of my dream, too, had now been fulfilled.

***

For years, the only thing I could do was adore my idols from a distance; the nearest I got was watching them on the TV or listening to radio commentaries. The experiences I had at school of being attacked by white boys and the pictures of hooligans fighting at football grounds and in the town centre on match days only served to increase my fear of going to a match. It would be a good few years before I set foot inside Old Trafford. Unfortunately, by then, all my idols had hung up their boots.

My ultimate humiliating football memory is watching, on the telly, the goal that relegated United to the then second division in 1974. Ironically, it was scored by none other than Dennis Law, playing for … Manchester City! How could you, Dennis?

Chapter 9

From Boy to Man

Like everyone else, I too wanted the different stages of my life to be a smooth and simple transitional process—to learn and grow with each stage. For me, the years piled up but made little or no difference to my confidence, self-esteem, or maturity. It would be an understatement to say I had led a very sheltered life. The death of my siblings and early illnesses led everyone around me to be overly protective, making allowances for me they probably would not have made for other children.

Even though my environment changed immensely when I came to England, my personality did not. During my teenage and early adulthood, in many ways, I remained the same shy unassuming boy. If anything, the older I got, the more I went into my shell. Apart from playing football, I found interaction with others difficult and conversations almost impossible.

As I look back, I am not seeking to blame anyone for how I was; I am simply trying to understand why I was that way. Let me share with you an example of how bad I have been, even as an adult.

By my late twenties, after leaving the bank and a short stint in the dairy I was now working on the buses. During breaks, I would go to the canteen, like everyone else. Unlike others, I usually sat by myself, avoiding having to talk to anyone. On one such occasion, an inspector walked in and sat down next to me. He then went to order his food. As he did so, I nervously and hurriedly put my food away and quickly walked out before he came back to the table. I simply could not handle having to talk to him, thinking I'd embarrass myself, even with simple conversations. For some reason, speaking to someone in authority was an added struggle. I just felt I couldn't cope. I have never understood why it was different when it came to those in authority. I coped well enough with passengers, as all they needed was a smile and for me to be polite.

I had become a young man who could be in the middle of a swinging party, where everyone else was having a wonderful time, chatting, eating, dancing, and simply having fun, whilst I sat alone. The same was true at family gatherings, where all were talking to each other, enjoying food, or just relaxing. Again, I would be sat in a corner, looking down, avoiding eye contact, deep in my thoughts. Yet, I would be hoping against hope that someone would talk to me, gently helping me to come out of the prison I had created for myself.

I worked my mundane job. That was it. There was no mischievous glint in my eye—no 'rocking the boat' of any sort, no risk-taking, no daring to have some fun or any sense of adventure. I remained the dutiful son, robotically doing what was asked of me.

Truth was, I was letting life pass me by without realising it was simply up to me to change things, to wake up and grab the moment. I simply didn't have it in me. Playing football was the only time I came alive. I only wish I could have used my passion for football to inspire me to do other things. Instead, I remained in a state of mind where I was waiting and hoping for something or someone to come along and shake me up. The reality is, I was totally incapable of thinking differently or freeing myself. It took a certain someone special to come along to do that.

Chapter 10

'Beta, You Are Getting Married'

In my twentieth year, I got my first job, with UBL. The following year, my parents had a conversation with me about something I 'd been dreading ever since I started work—getting married.

Most Asian children know who their parents have in mind for them when it comes to marriage. This tradition of 'arranged marriages' has been going on for centuries. I was considered old enough to do what all good Pakistani sons, or *betais*, were duty bound to do—settle down and marry. My parents had discussed who they had in mind for me. My father wanted someone from his side of the family; my mother, from hers. My father got his way, as was the case within the Pakistani community.

The wedding took place a month short of my twenty-first birthday, in October 1977. I married a very unfortunate young lady, Khalida Parveen, from Pakistan, a distant cousin. At the time, if asked about marriage, I would have said, 'No way.' I was incapable of such responsibility. However, I simply went along with my parents' wishes.

The prospect of getting married terrified me. Surely that's not how you should feel about starting a life with someone. I was very confused by the two different cultures I had grown up in—the traditional Pakistani culture and the more liberal one of my adopted country. I often wondered how good it must feel to be able to decide and choose for yourself who you wanted to marry and when. Despite my anxiety and discomfort, I told myself it was part of my duty to my parents; I could not cause them any more embarrassment. Despite feeling sorry for myself, I knew I had to accept my fate.

Unfortunately, when consumed with your own thoughts, it's easy to forget about other's feelings. If I'd managed to put aside mine for a moment, I may have considered what my parents were going through.

A couple who had taken a journey into the unknown, to a land where they faced many challenges, my parents had taken that step in the hope that their efforts may make life a little easier for their only surviving child. They came to this country in the hope of providing me opportunities for a better life. Now they were fulfilling the next part of their obligation—splashing out on my wedding.

The wedding was a nerve-racking affair. I couldn't stop worrying about every little thing. How do I greet guests? What if I mess up my lines? What if people don't like what I'm wearing? What if they don't like the food or the venue? What if, what if just kept going round and round in my head. I even thought about taking something to make myself ill, or worse. In the end, I did nothing.

As I recall, the wedding took place within a few weeks of my intended's arrival. According to our customs and tradition, the bride and groom were not allowed to see each other until the wedding day. That is how it was for us.

Mendhi nights were held for several evenings before the wedding, when there was hand and foot henna painting and lots of music, singing, and food. They were always organised and attended by women. I guess it was the Pakistani version of a hen do, although they would usually take place at the bride's house. Now, more and more of these are held at the same place as the wedding reception.

The wedding itself consisted of a religious ceremony, which took place in our local mosque. The imam asked us both if we willingly accepted the marriage; we both said yes. This was witnessed by at least two people. It was followed by a huge reception, as big and as lavish as the groom's parents could afford.

My reception took place in St Michael and All Saints Church on the corner of Palm Street and Whalley New Road, Blackburn. I could never have imagined my wedding or any Muslim wedding being held in a Christian place of worship. However, that thought never occurred to my parents; for them it was purely a case of economic necessity.

Throughout the reception, I sat still in the middle of the church hall, not daring to move or look up, not even to look at my new bride. I was frozen by fear. My one and only moment of happiness took place as the reception was coming to an end, when suddenly the whole of my team walked in. I knew they were playing a match, and I couldn't stop wondering how they were getting on. I wished I was with them. Their presence was both a welcome relief and a pleasant surprise.

My bride, Khalida, was a year younger than me, on paper at least. Just like me, she too had to have identity papers made hurriedly, once she found out she was going to England. Khalida is the eldest daughter of a distant cousin of my father's. Here was a young lady who had never been to school, brought up in the traditional way, to accept a way of life that was mapped out for her by her parents, her family, and her cultural norms. She'd learnt all the traditional skills of becoming a wife; a mother; and, more importantly, a good and dutiful daughter-in-law.

Khalida was and is an immensely kind and caring person. She left her family and came to England to marry, if not exactly a total stranger, someone she knew next to nothing about. In this respect, we were in the same boat. We had known each other as young children, having lived next door to each other. We'd heard rumours among the grown-ups that one day we would marry each other; this had a certain appeal that excited us as children. Such thoughts were soon forgotten when I first left for England.

To Khalida's immense credit, she accepted her fate, her marriage, and her new life exceptionally well. Not that we really talked about it, but I guess from her point of view, her life in this country would be a lot easier than the one in Pakistan.

Luckily, she hadn't come to England alone, as her younger sister Nasreen came with her. Nasreen married George . It was a joint wedding, which was a good thing for both sisters, as they provided each other with much-needed support.

Following the wedding, I slowly began to accept my fate and resigned myself to my married life as part of the duty of a loyal son. Over time, slowly, my selfish thoughts about a different kind of life started to subside.

Chapter 11

On the Buses!

After nearly three years with UBL, with my health deteriorating and my relationship with my new manager falling apart, it was inevitable that I'd need to look elsewhere for work. Although times were hard for most people, thankfully, jobs were plentiful, even for those with the most basic qualifications.

I left the bank in 1979 and became a bottler in a dairy, just outside Accrington. While this job didn't please my parents, they accepted it with their usual dignity and were more concerned about my health. Daisy Dairies was based in Oswaldtwistle. The job was repetitive and incredibly boring, yet at the same time, it was quite liberating. I no longer had the worry and anxiety of my previous job. Within weeks, I felt a great deal of weight lifted from my shoulders, and my stomach pains had stopped altogether.

It would be about this time that I bought my first car, a blue Hillman Avenger. The car was an absolute wreck; there is no way it would be allowed on the road today. One day, I was coming back from work with a friend, Gary, who I often gave a lift to. We were approaching the traffic lights at the Accrington Road/Shadsworth Road junction in Blackburn. The lights changed to red, and I went to brake, but the car just kept going. Fortunately, because of the condition of the car, I was driving well within the speed limit. Anticipating the lights would change, I had dropped from the fourth gear to the third. By applying the handbrake and changing down to first gear, the car eventually came to a halt—in the middle of the junction! Gary and I looked at each other and thanked our lucky stars that it was so quiet on the road.

Worse was to follow; after stopping, the damn thing stalled and wouldn't start again. Poor Gary had to push me all the way to his house, where we abandoned it. I eventually scrapped it and bought another, slightly better banger!

***

I'd only been working at the dairy for about three months when my brother-in-law, Amjid, returned to the United Kingdom from Denmark, after having lost his job as waiter in an Indian restaurant there. He started to look for work here. Amjid found a job he wanted to apply for, a bus conductor with Blackburn Transport, but he asked me to accompany him.

Although I already had a job and wasn't really looking for another one, once there, for some reason, I also applied. We filled in our application forms and were invited to an interview a few days later. Poor Amjid—he failed the interview. But I passed and decided to take the job. I became a bus conductor in April 1980.

In those days, you started as a bus conductor before training to become a bus driver. For someone who found it incredibly difficult to talk to people, I surprisingly loved being a bus conductor. Of course, there was the downside, as with any job—dealing with drunks, working late shifts, and finishing late. But constantly going up and down the stairs all day kept me fit, and I slowly started to enjoy talking to a few of the passengers, just basic stuff my shy personality allowed.

At first, I didn't have a regular driver. But within six months I was paired up with George (not his real name), a small, skinny man with a strong Scouse accent. He was originally from the Everton area of Liverpool and naturally supported the 'Toffees'. George was always very friendly towards all his colleagues. But surprisingly, he looked down on most of the passengers, calling them all sorts of horrible names. At the time, I found his behaviour confusing but lacked the confidence to tackle him about it.

Apart from that, we got on well and shared many a joke between us. Well, he told all the jokes—he had the gift of the gab. I just laughed. We also shared our love and passion for football and commiserated with each other, as neither of our teams came anywhere near challenging Liverpool's dominance.

Several other memories from my time on the buses come flooding back.

Despite being shy and self-conscious, I still approached life with a smile on my face and met many wonderful people. One was an elderly gentleman, who usually caught the bus from the Darwen terminus, opposite Darwen cemetery. Usually, he would travel to Darwen town centre. Sometimes, he would stay on the bus to Blackburn, to visit the library there. I could tell he was well read, even though we didn't get into any long conversations. He appeared a true gentleman, immaculately dressed and well groomed, always with a hat. He would always say, 'Good morning,' every time he got on the bus, with a beaming smile. And every time he got off, he'd say, 'Goodbye,' or, 'Thank you.' It's his immaculate manners that are etched in my mind, reminding me of my idol, Sir Bobby.

There were many others, perhaps not as distinguished as this gentleman but pleasant enough in their own way. On the other hand, there were one or two who were quite the opposite, especially after having consumed alcohol. This was often the case on the last bus, on several of our routes. Most of us suffered verbal abuse; some were even assaulted. On certain routes in Blackburn, thankfully the Darwen crew didn't do, a few had been threatened with a knife. The worst I had to endure were a few choice words.

I remember one character with great trepidation. Known by his nickname of 'Birdie', he was a big, burly man and was a huge Blackburn Rovers fan. He always caught the last bus from Blackburn town centre to Ewood Park every weekend. When sober, he was nice as pie and never stopped talking. However, when drunk, which was often, he would try to get away without paying. He often became abusive and aggressive when approached. In my earlier encounters, I found him intimidating and, like most of my colleagues, hesitated to approach him. But, like my colleagues, I soon figured him out and realised his bark was worse than his bite and insisted on making him pay his fare.

**

Talking of alcohol and pubs, I hadn't set foot in a pub until my mid-twenties. This was not unusual for most Muslims. Even though we'd been playing football for many years, very few of us ventured into pubs due to our religious beliefs. This came to a sudden end for me one day while at work.

I was on a late shift, working as a conductor with a new driver who liked to smoke his pipe, which was constantly in his mouth—even if it wasn't lit. We'd travelled from Blackburn to Darwen Cemetery, and just before reaching the terminus, he pulled up outside the Park Inn pub and asked if I could nip in and get him a box of matches; why we didn't stop outside a newsagent or a shop, I don't know.

I must have hesitated for a few moments, as he asked if I was OK. Without thinking, I said yes and very nervously got off the bus. Once inside the pub, for a split second, I froze with terror. I felt as if all eyes were on me, even though it wasn't busy, with only a few people scattered around the large bar area. I quickly went up to the bar, bought the box of matches, and rushed back onto the bus. I went to the back seat and sat down, shaking like a leaf. What was said to me by the barman, how much the matches cost, or if any other comments were made, I couldn't tell you. I was just relieved to be safely back on the bus.

I believe my overly fearful perceptions of pubs and alcohol, partly created by our lodger all those years ago, were reinforced by stories in the media of drunks causing chaos in pubs. In the pub, I felt that, at any moment, some drunk would attack me. Perceptions—or rather, misconceptions—can be dangerous, if unchecked. It took me many years to overcome my fear of pubs.

***

Other memories that stand out from working on the buses are of some of my colleagues. There was big Ricky Kirkland, a Scotsman, who was as loud as he was big, with a raucous laugh. He was certainly a big hit with the ladies. Ricky knew I was shy and would often tease me, especially about women.

However, I earned his respect on the football pitch following a goal I scored, lobbing him from the halfway line, whilst he was in goals!

Sorry Beckham/Rooney, my goal from the halfway line was a decade or two before either of yours.

Then there was Bill Hennessy, an Aussie. We first met after I qualified as a driver, and he became my regular conductor. On our early-morning shifts, Bill would always bring a flask of coffee, and I brought the biscuits—chocolate digestives were our favourites. I would put my foot down and get to the terminus as quickly as possible for our coffee and a 'biccy'. It was especially enjoyable on those cold, wintry mornings.

Bill and I became good friends away from the job. It was Bill who first piqued my interest in our beautiful countryside; we would often walk up to Darwen Tower (also known as Jubilee Tower), usually after our early shift. I remember the first time we went up; it was the middle of winter, with heavy snow everywhere. We didn't have any proper walking gear, not even boots, so we just wore our normal clothes and a heavy waterproof coat issued by Blackburn Transport. Walking through Sunny Hurst Woods to reach the tower was so peaceful, we forgot about the cold weather and hugely enjoyed the beautiful countryside.

Working with me as drivers and conductors were several other Asians, mainly Pakistanis; Blackburn Transport was certainly well represented by those from the Asian background. Like their white counterparts, I knew them all to talk to, but I would say I was closer to some of my white colleagues—mainly because of our shared love of football. Very few of my Asian colleagues played football, cricket being their main sport.

Chapter 12

Children: A Wonderful Gift of Life

Despite my feelings and reservations about my marriage, I had begun to accept my fate. I told myself this was how life was for me if I didn't want to hurt my parents. I told myself that perhaps the kind of happiness I was looking for was not meant for someone like me.

On 2 March 1979, Khalida gave birth to our first son, Mehboob. His birth shifted my focus towards him. He was a bundle of joy. He never stopped smiling, so much so that even my father, who hardly ever gave away his feelings or emotions, openly displayed his pride and joy, grinning from ear to ear. Mehboob's birth also alleviated my mother's anxiety about Khalida about grandchildren, even though we'd only been married for just over a year. Asian parents want grandchildren almost as soon as their children are married. I guess part of my mother's anxiety was related to when she lost her own first borns and when Khalida didn't become pregnant as soon as we were married, my mother became quite anxious.

Thankfully, we didn't have to wait long for our second child, another son. Bashir was born on 9 October 1980; incidentally, the names of my sons were chosen by my parents, as was the tradition in our Pakistani community.

I have to say I always wanted two children, and Bashir brought even more happiness and joy into our lives. They were both such happy-go-lucky toddlers. I remember coming home after a shift on the buses. Bashir would come bounding out of the back room towards me, shouting, 'My daddy is here, my daddy is here,' closely followed by the grinning Mehboob. They would lift my spirits and take away any other thoughts, running at me as soon as I walked through the front door. No matter how tired I felt, their smiling faces, their sparkling eyes, and their wonderful wholehearted embraces brought comfort to my weary body. They would jump on me and pull me one way and then another, falling, laughing, and doing it all over again.

With Mehboob and Bashir, I began to do the things I'd longed for with my father—simple things. We talked. I read to them, got down on the floor with them, had play-fights, made them laugh, and laughed with them. We went to the park, fed the ducks, kicked a ball about, and went for little drives together. Despite being shy and reserved, I found my sons brought out a playful more outgoing side of me.

I was surprised to learn that my cousins were not doing the same with their children. They were still restricted by our cultural norms. In that respect, my sons had set me free. We openly demonstrated our feelings and emotions to each other.

Sometimes in life, in moments of joy, we get the urge to do things we wouldn't normally do—silly, daft things that aren't part of our normal behaviour. One such behaviour happened one late evening; after finishing my last journey, instead of taking my bus directly to the depot, I took a little detour. It had been a long day, and I was missing my sons. To my surprise, they were still up but were in their pyjamas. I had meant to just see them before taking the bus to the depot, but as soon as I saw their glowing and excited faces, I decided to take them for a little bus ride. I was overcome with the sheer joy of seeing them and made a rash decision in the heat of the moment. I loved every minute of the wonderfully joyous expression on their faces. In a more rational state of mind, I would never have done that.

Even now, I get so excited just thinking about that time when Mehboob and Bashir were sitting on the darkened bus, smiling away. When in their company, all my anxieties and insecurities seemed to disappear. My daydreaming moments only took place when I was on my own—and that only happened when they were tucked up in bed.

Our life together was wonderful, and we were as happy as any father and his children could be. Unfortunately, life has a way of showing you how unpredictable it can be. What took place next shattered Mehboob and Bashir's young lives. They were only eight and six, respectively, when my life took an unexpected turn towards a very selfish direction.

I walked out on them!

My decision put me on a long path of self-discovery and self-gain. But at the same time, it had a devastating and destructive impact on their lives, so immense they are still recovering from it today—over thirty years later.

At the time, I never truly realised the devastating effect my decision would have on them. Before they were born, I used to spend hours thinking about how, when I had children, their lives would be different from mine. They wouldn't spend hour upon hour in their rooms alone with no one to talk to, nobody to share their thoughts with, play with, or confide in. I would be the 'father-friend' to them I had yearned for.

It took me years to realise that, by leaving them, I took away all the things I'd said I would provide for them. From the bright happy-go-lucky young boys they were, they grew into shy and introverted young men. A sad 'little-boy-lost' look became constant in their eyes. I had become the father I'd promised I would never be—a father whose children became so distant from him they found it difficult even to talk to him. Worse still, I became a father they feared.

We all know that we make rational decisions when the head is in control, when we give more thought to the needs of others than to our own. At that time, my heart ruled my head. I could only see what I needed to make myself happy, without realising the damage I would cause my sons.

Fortunately, due to that bit of spark that has remained within both my sons and the upbringing provided by their grandparents and despite their fear of me, they have allowed me to maintain a relationship with them. Years of pain and sorrow have caused them both deep scars, which we all understand will take a long time to heal. To their credit, Mehboob and Bashir's willingness to forgive and make amends amazes me. They are slowly beginning to understand what happened to our lives, why I took the decision to walk out on them, and my desire to find my own personal happiness and some meaning to my life. I am not sure that, were I in their position, I would have been able to do that so readily.

Not only do I have understanding and forgiving parents, but my sons too. I am an extremely fortunate man.

Mehboob, Bashir, you are so very special.

Chapter 13

'Race You': A Chance Meeting That Changed My Life!

What happened next in my life is something that only existed in the deepest recesses of my imagination. It eclipsed all my dreams, even surpassing that of playing alongside Sir Bobby or scoring the winning goal for United in the Champions League Final. Nevertheless, it was a reoccurring dream when I was floating on my special go-to cloud, escaping from reality.

Dreaming about falling in love with someone was one thing, but the possibility of it happening to me was quite another. It was silly of me to even imagine it. I was a Pakistani Muslim, dutiful and married. What was the matter with me? How could I even have such thoughts?

I knew having those thoughts was fantasy and wrong. In a strange way, I felt sooner or later, I would be punished for having such 'bad' thoughts. Yet, though you know it's wrong, you still can't help thinking of such thoughts.

Falling in love was not something that was permitted or common in my culture. The need for courtship was negated by the tradition of arranged marriages. There is usually a very heavy price to pay for those who defy cultural norms. Alienation by the family and the community is often the first step; it can also lead to threats and violent attacks. Tragically, there have also been cases of young people paying the ultimate price—killed by family members to protect the family 'honour'. In those days, it was not surprising that very few young people went against their upbringing and cultural norms. Now, times are changing, with more young people marrying someone of their choice.

I had been married for just over nine years and had been working on the buses since 1980, when, in 1986, on an otherwise ordinary day, something extraordinary took place.

***

Six years after I started with Blackburn Transport, the company decided to make changes to our existing route. At the time, Blackburn Transport had two depots—one in Intack and one on Blackburn Road, Darwen. I was based in the Darwen depot.

Until the route changes, Darwen staff operated all the routes in Darwen and only the main Blackburn to Darwen Cemetery route in Blackburn. The changes meant that this route was extended from Blackburn bus station to the terminus at Wilpshire. The extension, approximately three miles long, took in one of the most affluent areas of Blackburn.

Although Wilpshire was less than three miles from Bastwell, where I lived, it seemed a million miles away when it came to the lifestyles of the two groups of residents. Residents in Wilpshire were white, affluent, and upwardly mobile. Bastwell's residents were mainly working class, with one of the highest concentrations of Asian populations in Lancashire and similar inner-city challenges faced in many northern towns and cities.

If these route changes hadn't taken place, I believe I would have remained a bus driver for the rest of my working life.

The extension turned it into one of our best routes. Passengers on this route were friendly, polite, and courteous. We rarely had to deal with drunks, even on the last bus.

For me, this extension to our route meant much, much more.

***

In the 1980s, when I joined Blackburn Transport, most drivers did their shift as a driver and then, for overtime, did a few hours as a conductor. There seemed to be plenty of overtime for conductors but hardly any for drivers, as most conductors went on to become drivers.

One day, soon after being on this route, I was working as a conductor, grabbing as much overtime as possible. After collecting fares on the top deck, I came downstairs—and that was when I first saw her; immediately, she took my breath away. As I approached her, she gave me a warm smile, and I said, 'Yes please.'

She had long dark brown permed hair, and she appeared tall, even when sat down. She was slim, with greyish blue eyes that danced and sparkled and were impossible to avoid, even for someone so shy. She had an incredible smile, which simply melted my heart. I was totally blown away. For once in my shy and nervous life, I held my gaze and did not look away. For a few moments, I was mesmerised.

'Town centre please,' she said confidently and clearly.

'Thirty-six pence please,' I said politely.

There was nothing further said, apart from a thank you when she got off. But for days, I could not stop thinking about her—going over every spoken word, recalling her gorgeous smile and every little detail I could, trying desperately to find any signs of encouragement. For days, I thought of what I might do or say if I saw her again. All sorts of different thoughts went through my head. *I could talk about the weather—English people like talking about the weather. No. What am I thinking? Why would anyone, let alone someone like her, even look to me?*

This torment went on for days. As eagerly as I wanted to, I didn't see her again for days. Days turned into weeks, my anguish growing with every passing hour. Six or seven weeks must have passed when, one day, while heading to our next stop on Ainsworth Street from Blackburn Boulevard, I caught a glimpse of her.

I was standing at the front of the bus and talking to the driver—we were waiting for the lights to change—when I saw her running towards the bus stop on Ainsworth Street. I was so caught up in my thoughts, thinking about what I would say when she hopped on the bus in front, to my utter dismay, she vanished as quickly as she appeared. That damn bus was running late! As we got to Ainsworth Street, I was so disappointed, my heart still pounding, only to be jolted from my thoughts by the driver who asked, 'Are you all right?'

All right?! No, of course I wasn't all right. How could I be? But I couldn't say that to him, so I just smiled politely.

As we had to stick to our timetable, by the time we got to the terminus, there was no sign of her. All sorts of thoughts went through my head as I went to sit at the back of the bus. I was being punished for even thinking about another woman. *I am married. Shame on me.* Yet, despite this, despite all the reasons not to think about her, I simply couldn't stop myself.

When I was at home, Mehboob and Bashir brought back some kind of normality to my life. Their innocent faces would help me focus on them and push any other thoughts away, temporarily.

It would be precisely three months, two weeks, and four days before I saw her again. By this time, the company had switched to one-person operators, meaning we no longer had conductors.

At precisely the right time, I left Wilpshire terminus for the return journey to Blackburn. At the very next stop, there was only one passenger waiting to get on.

Is it? Could it be? Yes, yes, it is. My heart immediately began to race. *Keep calm and breathe,* I told myself.

'Good morning. Thirty-six pence please,' she said.

'Good morning,' I replied.

'Lovely weather we're having,' she said.

It really is true what they say about the British and the weather, I thought.

'How are you enjoying the new route? Some of the drivers don't seem so keen,' she went on, probably sensing my nervousness.

They must be mad, I said to myself and then managed to get a few words out. 'I think this route makes a lovely change to our usual boring one,' I finally said.

'Oh good. Thank you.' She took her ticket and then sat down at the front of the bus—just where I was hoping she would.

I took every opportunity to look at her, quickly looking away in case she caught me staring. She got off in town and very politely said, 'Thank you.'

I was to see her three or four more times when she caught my bus, displaying that wonderful smile of hers, when something quite extraordinary happened. I would not have believed it if it hadn't happened to me.

It was the height of summer and we had by then become conductorless. I was at the bus stop on Ainsworth Street, and a queue of passengers was waiting to get on. I quickly scanned the queue for her, but there was no sign of her. I then went on 'autopilot', issuing tickets and becoming oblivious to anything else.

Suddenly, I heard a tap on the driver's window. Startled, I turned away from the boarding passengers towards the driver's window. I couldn't believe what I saw. There she was, in the middle of the road, on her bicycle, leaning against the bus with that fabulous smile and those dancing eyes.

She was dressed in a sleeveless cotton pink top and white cotton shorts that looked more like football shorts. My heart started pounding. She saw the surprised and confused look on my face, and calmly said, 'Race you to the terminus,' and then shot off.

For a few seconds, I was left dumbfounded, small beads of sweat forming on my forehead. There was a look of equal bewilderment on the faces of the passengers as they got on, but none of them said anything. After the last of the passengers had boarded, I set off. I did my best to remain calm but wondered if that had really happened. I overtook her a couple of times before she finally overtook me and disappeared from my view just past Roe Lee, assuring me it really did happen.

I got to the Brownhill bus stop, a couple of stops from the terminus, where most of the passengers were getting off. I remember thinking, *please hurry. I need to get to the terminus.* I was worried that, if I took too long, she would have disappeared again.

Just as the last few passengers were getting off, I heard a tap on the driver's window.

There she was again, leaning against the bus in the middle of the road. As I slid open the window, she looked at me and said, 'Have a drink. You must be really hot.' She handed me a can of lemonade shandy.

I nearly fell off my seat. I can't imagine what the passengers thought. As someone who found making eye contact difficult, I just didn't know where to look or what to do. I had no idea what to say. I was certainly not expecting that!

I simply muttered, 'No ... no. I'm fine. Thank you.'

'Go on. You look so hot. This'll cool you down,' she insisted.

What could I say? On the one hand, I was flattered that a gorgeous woman was offering me a drink; on the other, I felt embarrassed. On top of that, the drink was alcoholic and against my religion, so I couldn't drink it. There were still some passengers getting off; as polite as they were, they didn't half give me some strange looks. The sort of person I was in those days, I just wanted the ground to open and swallow me.

Picture the scene. A beautiful woman in a T-shirt and shorts is leaning against the outside of my bus, offering me a drink. I'm thinking, *I've died and gone to heaven! Surely this isn't real?*

Oh, but it was real. The vision is so vividly ingrained in my brain. I light up every time I think about it.

She sensed my embarrassment and quickly said, 'OK, even if you won't have a drink, I'm still going to beat you to the terminus.' And with that, she shot off.

As she sped away, a sobering thought occurred to me, and I remember saying to myself, *well done, you prat. You've certainly blown that!*

At the last stop before the terminus, as the last remaining passengers were getting off, an elderly gentleman leaned in towards me and said, 'You have an incredibly spirited young lady there, you lucky devil.' He then winked and walked off. He obviously thought we were together or married; otherwise, surely no woman would have the audacity to do what she had just done.

When I got to the terminus, much to my relief, she was standing beside her bike, waiting.

'What kept you?' she said with a mischievous grin.

Folks, please meet Marge—the English rose I was destined to meet. Marjorie Alice Hocking, her full name, was the woman who was to bring much personal happiness and joy into my life, the woman who would devote her life to helping me become the man I am today. We still both have a giggle when we reminisce about how we met and what happened in the middle of Whalley New Road, Blackburn, all those years ago.

Today, over thirty years later, our love for each other burns brighter than ever.

Try as hard as I may, I know that everything I share about Marge is tainted by someone totally smitten with her. However, we have had some great adventures together that I never thought would come my way.

Marge and I are so opposite that whoever said 'opposites attract' clearly knew that some people can be extremely opposite to each other and yet be so right for each other. I think you already have a fair idea of what I was like in those days. Well, this gorgeous lady was nothing like me at all. Where I was cautious and safe, she was adventurous. Where I was subdued, she was bubbly. Where I dared not take a risk, she would not even consider it a risk. Where I struggled to put a few words together, conversation flowed from her with ease.

The words that came out of Marge's mouth were sweet music to my ears. On top of all that, Marge has one of those hearty laughs, expressed with a fantastic sense of freedom. Her eyes and face light up, infecting everyone around her, compared with my cautious and uncertain smile, limited by fear and doubt.

As different as we were, there was an instant and undeniable chemistry that was far stronger and more enduring, irrespective of our backgrounds. We instantly felt a deeper connection that would help with the many challenges that were to come our way.

But first, let me take you back to that day of the 'race'. As you can imagine, I was completely overwhelmed by what had just happened. Yet, for some unexplained reason, and for the first time in my life, I was not as nervous as I should have been.

Marge leant her bike against the hedge and came onto the bus. With a little prompting and deliberate openings for me, conversation between us slowly began to flow. We arranged to meet again, very soon.

A Game of Squash

Just two days later, Marge caught my bus home from the town centre. At the terminus, we spoke for a few minutes; she could tell I was more nervous this time. She quickly found something I enjoyed talking about, sport, and following a few words on football, Marge asked if I played squash. I didn't, but said I wanted to learn. She agreed to teach me.

On my day off the following week, we agreed to meet. In the days leading up to our meeting, I began to wonder if she would really turn up. Or would it turn out to be just another of my dreams? Thankfully, she did. I picked her up not far from where she lived, and she took me to a squash club called Cloggers in Little Harwood. Unfortunately, the club is no longer there, but the date is forever etched in my mind, 26 September 1986, our first date.

How did the game of squash go? I could hardly hit the ball— not just because I hadn't played squash before or lacked eye-to-ball coordination, but quite simply because I couldn't take my eyes off her legs! But as we started to play regularly, I fell in love with squash too. In fact, later, as my ankles began to give up on me, making it difficult to continue playing football, I turned to squash more and more.

However, our courtship was not so straightforward. Our racial, cultural, social, and economic backgrounds posed some challenges. Rarely could the odds be stacked up so high against two people who wanted to be together. On top of that, I was married and still had my head in the clouds. Marge was going through the process of her separation and divorce. With our overwhelming feelings for each other, we were determined to overcome our challenges and began to see each other more and more. I guess we adopted the 'us against the world' mentality.

It was not long after we started to see each other that Blackburn Transport decided to shut down its Darwen depot, moving all staff to the Blackburn depot at Intack. It made no difference to us. On the late shifts, Marge would catch my bus leaving Wilpshire terminus, which would be the last bus from Blackburn to Darwen. She would remain on the bus as I drove it to the depot, getting off just before the depot and waiting for me nearby. We would then spend precious moments walking home together.

Sometimes, Marge would come to meet me at the depot on her bicycle. I sat on the seat as she pedalled us home—not something I could ever have imagined in my wildest dreams. Surely such simple pleasures were for films, not for a Pakistani man like me!

A silver wig and a miniskirt

Every time I met Marge, it was like going on a new and exciting adventure. Falling in love and the courtship is hugely exciting in itself— but falling in love when it's forbidden is even more thrilling. Marge was bringing so much joy into my life. Seeing her made me smile—not my usual kind of insecure, uncertain smile. No, this was different. It was a genuine smile that only comes when your heart is lit up. Despite everything we have gone through, over the years, that smile comes to me so readily every time I look at Marge.

I remember once when she got on my bus at Wilpshire, she was wearing a short dress and a silver wig. The outfit was befitting someone brave enough to stand in the middle of the road, lean against the driver's window, and offer him a drink, ignoring what anyone else thought. She looked stunning.

I picked her up at Wilpshire for my last journey from Blackburn to Darwen. There were no other passengers where she got on. She gave me her fabulous smile, we exchanged a few words, and she went to sit on the back seat. There were only a handful of passengers who got on during the journey into town. For the last bus from Blackburn to Darwen, only about a dozen passengers boarded, which was low for the last bus. These passengers included one young man who went to sit on the back seat, next to Marge. Though I didn't like that, there was little I could do.

When we set off from the boulevard, I kept a constant eye on the back seat. I could see a conversation going on between them, making me anxious and somewhat uncomfortable.

At Ewood Park, the young man came to the front to get off. As he waited for me to stop the bus, he looked back at Marge and said, 'Are you sure now?'

To this, she simply smiled and nodded.

All the way to Darwen, I kept wondering what he could have meant by that. When we got to Darwen and after everyone had gotten off but before I could get a word out, Marge simply said, 'He was trying to chat me up and wanted to take me home. I did think about it but decided against it.' She looked at me with a twinkle in her eyes.

Having little or no sense of humour in those days, I honestly didn't know whether she was joking or serious, until she gave me that wonderful reassuring smile of hers.

We continued to meet this way or with Marge coming to meet me at the depot on her bike. Riding home on her bike seemed so wrong in so many ways, and yet so right, so exciting and exhilarating.

During the many, many times we walked or rode together like this, it almost always rained, or it was extremely cold, with heavy snow. However, on some nights, the moon and stars came out, shining brightly, reminding me of my childhood and playing hide-and-seek in Pakistan. I was playing a different hide-and-seek game now. Marge had brought the stars and the moonlight back into my life.

Blanket on the ground

In our early days, it was convenient for us to meet after I finished work, late at night. However, a short time later, just like most people smitten with each other, we wanted to see more of each other and at different times. We, therefore, began to meet on some of my days off. This was of course difficult to explain at home; after all, there was only a limited number of times I could use 'working overtime', 'going on a protest march', or 'going out with some friends' before my family suspected something was wrong.

If thinking of excuses for coming home late or spending more time away on my days off was not enough, where to go without being seen was also a problem. For this, I totally relied on Marge, having had no experience or understanding of a man's role during courtship. At times, quite rightly, this would frustrate Marge, as it would any woman. Some women, perhaps from the older group, want their man to take responsibility, to take them to nice places and wine and dine them. Unfortunately, such things were alien to me.

Yes, I know. What was a sophisticated lady like Marge doing with someone like me? Her answer, when I asked years later, was quite simple, 'There was enough about you for me to want to be with you.'

Not exactly the ingredients for a great relationship, you might think. I genuinely believe that many women in her position would have sent me packing. Not Marge, she persevered. Although to tease me, she would say, 'You were a real pain in the neck, as I felt I had to teach you everything,' before smiling and adding, 'But there was something about you that I wanted in my life.' She saw something in me that no one else had seen, not even me.

What also helped us a great deal was Marge's love for the countryside. She certainly opened my eyes to a world beyond Whalley Range and Bastwell, the odd trip to Blackpool or the family visits to Bradford. Although I enjoyed the countryside, my only experience of our wonderful countryside was the walks to Darwen Tower, with my Australian bus conductor.

With Marge's patience and tender support, we started to explore the beauty of nearby places in Lancashire. Such places as the Trough of Bowland; Chipping, Whalley, and Clitheroe; Pendle Hill; the Longridge fells; Jeffrey Hill near Longridge; and the coastal towns of Lytham, Fleetwood, and Morecombe became our frequent destinations. So much wonderful natural beauty was so close, yet so far from the world I'd lived in before I met Marge.

In due course, we began to travel beyond Lancashire. We would go walking in the Lake District. We travelled to the Snowdonia National Park, catching a train up to the summit of Snowdon—something I did later with Mehboob and Bashir. Our favourite of all was Scotland, with regular drives past Fort William and Ben Nevis to Mallaig, Inverness, around Loch Lomond and to Braemar, Stirling, and Edinburgh.

We will never forget the wonderful and warm welcome we received from Mrs McAllister (not her real name), the owner of a bed and breakfast in Braemar. It was late at night, with all pubs and cafés closed, yet the dear old lady made us a delicious Scottish meal.

Such beautiful places were another world to the one I was living in—or rather, drifting along in. Of course, I am not claiming to be a Walter Scott. But slowly, Marge began to expand my horizons.

One such occasion was when, again late at night, we were enjoying being parked up on Jeffery Hill, near Longridge, after spending the afternoon driving around the Trough of Bowland. Most evenings in winter, Jeffery Hill is covered in thick fog and mist, ideal for courting couples. We were in some state of undress, with a large blanket over us both. We had had a late lunch but no tea, so were feeling hungry.

Suddenly, we decided to get some food and headed off to the Little Chef, (now closed) on the A6 in Bilsborough.

We drove all the way there with that blanket around us, in our underwear! It is not something either of us would've normally dared do or have done since. None of my friends believed me when I told them what I had done. It was purely a spur of the moment thing. We dressed in the Little Chef's car park before having some fish and chips for supper. Just like Billie Jo Spears's famous song, this was our version of 'blanket on the ground'!

Meet the family

Marge and I had been seeing each other for around a year when we discussed introducing each other to our families. However, we both agreed, for a variety of reasons, that it was simply out of the question for Marge to meet my family. Even after twelve months, we decided meeting my family was a step too far for everyone, as I was still married and making up excuses when seeing Marge.

We agreed for me to meet Marge's parents one evening after work. At the time, Jack and Phyllis Wadsworth lived on Tulketh Brow (no. 48), near Lane Ends, Preston. Both were retired. Jack had worked as a gas fitter for the gas board, while Phyllis had always been a housewife. Jack had fought in the Second World War as a royal engineer. For his age, Jack was in good health; however, Phyllis always seemed to be in bed, suffering from chronic back pain and other ailments, including diabetes. Meeting Jack and Phyllis remains a vivid recollection in my mind.

That evening, I picked Marge up at one of our agreed rendezvous points and drove to Preston. When we got there, Marge asked me to wait in the car, as she hadn't told her parents about me or that we were coming over to see them together. As I waited, several things went through my mind. She probably didn't tell them because her dad would 'flip'. Jack was from an era in which many thought it was totally wrong to get divorced, let alone get involved with a married Pakistani man, of all people.

Marge had only been gone a few minutes; those few minutes were enough for my mind to race away with all sorts of thoughts. What if they don't want to see me? What if they don't like me? What do I say to them? How do I behave? My nervousness and anxiety were beginning to get the better of me. I was relieved to see Marge walk back to the car and take me in to meet her parents.

As I went through the front door, Jack was on the phone in the hallway. When Marge introduced me, he completely blanked me. I can imagine how I may have appeared to him. If he had looked up, he would have seen an awkward-looking young man, not knowing what to do, constantly looking towards his daughter for reassurance. I'm sure it probably made whatever impression he had of me even worse—not exactly an ideal way to impress your girlfriend's father!

Picking up on my awkwardness, Marge took me into the living room at the rear of the house to see her mum. Phyllis gave me a beaming smile and a long embrace and gestured for me to sit next to her. As the conversation flowed, Phyllis even joked and asked if I was sure about taking on her 'wild one', as she referred to her eldest daughter. Phyllis's natural warmth and friendliness helped to calm my nerves, made worse following Jack's response. Naturally, we had a cup of tea and a slice of cake—Victoria sponge with strawberry jam, as I recall. It was the first time I had ever had Victoria sponge cake.

The welcome by Phyllis was in complete contrast to her husband. After his telephone conversation, he came into the living room but never said a word to me. Both Phyllis and Marge made excuses for him, saying he hardly said a word to anyone, preferring to read his books.

I had experienced racism as a child during my school days. But as an adult I'd been extremely fortunate, even throughout the height of racist tensions during the late 1970s and early 1980s. I had faced little direct racism that some from my community had suffered.

However, having been introduced to Jack, it felt as if racism was now staring me right between the eyes. It was not something I could avoid. Fortunately, in time and due to continued visits, I managed to change Jack's attitude towards me. I was helped by Marge's persistence, her mum's 'rollicking' of Jack, and what usually happens over a period time when human beings are thrust together.

Something usually gives; the relationship either breaks down completely or a bond slowly develops. As with Shantilal all those years ago, a slow bond developed between Jack and me. Our preconceived thoughts about each other were pushed away by our curiosity to learn about and from each other. Slowly but surely, Jack began to see beyond the colour of my skin. Both Marge and Phyllis did everything they could to make sure Jack and I spent as much time together as possible. On every visit, they engineered opportunities for us to be left alone with each other, slowly starting conversations between us.

Women are such creative creatures.

With Jack, even in my blissful ignorance, I soon became aware that he had preconceived ideas about Asian people. But once I was able to deal with those, it was only a matter of time before he realised, he had no basis for disliking me. This is how it proved to be; over time, he began to treat me better than his own sons. Jack and I became remarkably close—in many ways, I was closer to Jack than to my own father. Jack took me to watch him play crown green bowling. He also taught me to play chess, albeit rather badly, as I never beat him.

For some reason Jack was under the impression that I owned a bus company, rather than merely drove one. When I asked him if owning a bus company made any difference to him, he simply said, 'No, but I would have enjoyed free bus rides.' I soon realised he would always try to make light of most situations.

My relationship with Jack also reinforced in me never to be too hasty in judging people and to try and get beyond the 'front' that some people put on. It was a valuable lesson to learn and immensely helpful in my later career.

A sign of how good our relationship had become was when he gave me his prized set of crown green bowls, or 'woods' as he called them, shortly before he passed away.

Through regularly visiting Marge's parents, I got to hear about and met most of her family—her brothers Peter and Stephen, her sisters Jackie and Sue, and Sue's husband Joan Ramon, 'JR'. Over the years, we have become close to Sue and JR, who live in Spain, enjoying their generous hospitality on several occasions.

Then, there was, of course, our auntie Barb, Phyllis's younger sister, who also lives in Spain. I had already met Marge's daughter, Jane, and son, Simon, within months of us going out with each other. Jane was incredibly friendly, accepting of me from the start; with Simon, it took a little while before we also became very close.

Decision time

Being with Marge preoccupied my mind most of the time. I even started to miss several football games, totally unthinkable for me.

There was a lot to think through though. As great as it was being with Marge, coming home and having to leave her was becoming more and more difficult. On many occasions when I got in, often following a late shift, my parents would still be up, and I would have to lie to them, again and again. The lying was tearing me apart. I couldn't bear to look them in the eye.

Their one and only son was doing what no one could ever have imagined. I was on a path that could only bring them pain and shame. I was now the son who was about to shatter their world to pieces.

My wife had stopped waiting up for me, realising, gradually, that we had become distanced and that there was something irretrievably wrong. In her gentle and totally dutiful Pakistani way, she would tell me what I was doing was wrong and yet still carried on looking after me, my parents, and our children.

I was desperate to talk to someone, to share my thoughts and feelings, to get some advice. But who could I turn to? I thought no one would understand my predicament; they'd only say how wrong it was and that I was letting my parents down. I couldn't escape such thoughts, which were weighing heavy on my mind. I couldn't even tell Marge. If she knew about the turmoil I was in, she would have taken the decision out of my hands and ended our relationship. I would have lost her forever, and I certainly didn't want that.

Looking back, I'm amazed that Marge did stay with me, which has everything to do with her patience and strength of character and little to do with me.

But a decision was needed; I could not go on like this.

Mahmood Ahmed

Move to Preston

In 1987, Marge decided to leave her marital home to live on her own. She felt it would be better for her to make a complete break and move away from Blackburn but still be close enough for her children.

She moved into a flat above a launderette, 25 Blackpool Road, Ribbleton, Preston. Her new residential area was in complete contrast to her home in Wilpshire. However, by sheer coincidence, it wasn't too far from the area she grew up in. But how it had changed over the years. Recalling her memories of her neighbourhood of yesteryear, she would tell me how clean it had been, how people had smiled and chatted to each other, with all the time in the world. She described family and community life in the fifties and sixties, so laid-back and different from the couldn't-care-less attitude of many people today.

Marge and I had now been seeing each other for just over eighteen months, and we could no longer continue living apart or telling our families more lies. We decided that, if our feelings meant anything, we needed to be together.

Within months of Marge's move to Preston, I too left my family home and moved in with her. For many years, I never realised the full impact of walking out on my family, especially on my sons. I was so naive and wrapped up in my own selfish needs. The full extent of the impact is something they are still recovering from. If not for Marge's love and me slowly finding the man hidden deep inside, I'm not sure I would have been able to cope with the full extent of what I had done.

After I left, Mehboob, although much quieter than his brother, stopped showing his feelings, emotions, or his ready smile altogether. In this aspect, he was and is very much like me. Yet, as I have mentioned previously, he was not like that before I left. My memories of him are of an ever-so-happy child.

Bashir, on the other hand, was different, openly displaying his feelings and emotions. My leaving has had such a profound effect on them both, and years of life without me has drained Bashir of his energy and zest for life. He, like his brother, has sunk into a place riddled with confusion, self-doubt, and self-blame. Their glittering and happy eyes have been replaced with eyes that are sad and sorrowful.

It is only in recent years that we've begun to come to terms with those 'vacant' years. Now married, a lot of their happiness is down to their wives—both, coincidently, called Sadia—as well the three of us having some meaningful and quality time together, slowly opening up about the hurt I caused them.

There was a lot about my culture I rebelled against. However, if it wasn't for the influence of the traditional Pakistani culture, then rebuilding any kind of relationship with my two sons would have been incredibly difficult, maybe even impossible. Both Mehboob and Bashir are naturally kind and caring people, but along their grandparents' and their mother's good influence, it is also their culture that has taught them to respect their elders. This respect has taught them to be incredibly tolerant and patient with me, helping them to readily forgive me for abandoning them and to try and understand my selfish actions.

They say separation and divorce is easier and much more accepted within Western society. Or is that just my perception? The reality for us has been somewhat different, particularly for Marge. Before her separation and divorce, she had a large pool of friends, people she knew and socialised with. However, when she moved out of her marital home, that all changed. One by one, she lost them all. We've often wondered why that might be. Was it her divorce? Or was it because she had set up home with me? We will never know.

For different reasons, moving into our new home together was a massive reality check for us both. Marge had lived in a large, detached house in an affluent area. She was now living in a one-bedroom flat in a run-down area of Preston, a stark contrast from her previous lifestyles, and it took her a little while to get used to it. To her credit, the way she took it all in her stride, without moaning, is a measure of the woman she is.

As much as I wanted to be with Marge and start our new life together, leaving Mehboob and Bashir behind, letting my parents down, and turning Khalida's world upside down was not easy to deal with. On top of all that, for the first few months in our new home, we were welcomed by a brick through our window almost every other weekend. It was a sign of how some in that area viewed mixed-race relationships.

'Member of the Yellow Peril Brigade': A pathway to a new career

After making the decision to move to Preston, Marge and I discussed what I should consider as my next job. I was quite happy working as a bus driver, but it was totally impractical to live in Preston and travel to Blackburn to work shifts. I also started to bounce around in my head the idea of finding a daytime job, which would allow me to study in the evenings. I hadn't quite figured out what I would study; perhaps I'd resit my O levels and look at what computer courses were available.

What I took for my next job was a total surprise to both of us. Searching the classifieds in the local paper, I found an advert in the *Lancashire Evening Post* for wardens. Initially, we both dismissed it.

Then, following further discussions and as a 'stopgap', I decided to apply.

Much to my surprise and following what I thought was a lengthy recruitment process, I was successful. In April 1988, I officially became a member of the 'Yellow Peril Brigade', a traffic warden with Lancashire Constabulary.

What on earth possessed a mild-mannered, quietly spoken shy man to consider one of the most hated jobs? I hear you ask. To be perfectly honest, I'm not totally sure. The fact that I had few qualifications and virtually no skills left me with very few options. But the new job would leave my evenings free, allowing me to study. Marge was always telling me I could do better, and I slowly began to think that, perhaps, I could find something that would stretch my brain a little more and the new job would be a steppingstone.

As a traffic warden, I worked from within a police station, based on Lawson Street in the centre of Preston. (The station has long since closed, with all the staff rehoused in their brand-new, purpose-built premises on Lancaster Road North). Working out of a police station and having regular contact with police officers, I became interested in what they did. A few of them made time for me and provided a good insight into their role. Up to that point, and with what little I knew about the police service, the thought of becoming a police officer could not have been further from my mind.

Now, following detailed conversations with several police officers, a new career path was about to open for me.

Part II

My Career with Lancashire Constabulary

Chapter 14

My Son: 'A Poleeceman'

After eighteen months of being everyone's favourite traffic warden, I was becoming bored with constantly doing the same thing, issuing tickets to irresponsible motorists. The more I learned about the role of a police officer, the more it appealed to me. It also fitted in with what my father had told me about 'being of service to others', something I would always aspire to. Furthermore, it was much more aligned to my deep-rooted sense of fairness and seeking justice for those unable to do so for themselves.

When considering this huge step, my first port of call for advice should have been the woman always by my side. But I chose not to do that. I don't know why. Perhaps I wanted to prove a point to myself, or perhaps, naively, to show Marge I was now ready to do things for myself.

Anyway, I decided to speak to one of the police inspectors, a brave move, considering my fear of those in authority. Unfortunately, I found the inspector to be unfriendly and unhelpful—the same inspector, by the way, who went on to become deputy chief constable in another force. He abruptly told me not to bother. 'You're too old. Stick to being a traffic warden,' was his advice. At the time, being as naive as I was, I thought no more of it and left it at that.

Now, having retired from the police service, with many years of experience in the policing environment and culture behind me, I cannot help but feel that perhaps the inspector's motives were tinged with prejudice. If he had wanted to help, he could easily have found out about the recruitment process and the upper age limit or at least pointed me in the right direction.

With my tail between my legs and my already low confidence battered, I finally spoke to Marge about it. After giving me a pep talk, she encouraged me to contact the recruitment department. Luckily, I didn't have to. Whilst still contemplating this, the recruitment team visited Preston police station as part of their internal recruitment drive. They were seeking to encourage civilian police staff to apply for police officer roles. They provided me with all the relevant information about the recruitment process and the criteria, including the upper age limit, which was thirty-five. I was thirty-two—phew!

In most humans, there is an innate kindness and trustfulness, which I used to have; it can come from naivety and innocence, which are great in an ideal world. My first hard lesson was given to me by that inspector—we don't live in an ideal world. I needed to change if I was going to survive as a police officer.

Naivety and innocence are qualities that Mehboob and Bashir and my stepson, Simon, all have—appealing qualities that, on the one hand, I desperately want them to keep. They are endearing qualities, which makes them caring towards other people and trusting of them. On the other hand, I fear this increasingly selfish world will take advantage of them. I am fearful of the painful lessons they'll have to learn—wishing as all parents do to be able to protect from such harsh lessons .

***

Before applying to become a police officer, I also sought views from my friends and some members of my community, hoping to assure myself of doing the right thing. I wish I hadn't bothered. The vast majority wanted me to avoid the police service at all costs; for most of them, the police service was intrinsically racist. They said an Asian would never fit in and stated, 'There is a reason why there are so few Asians within the police force.'

In the past, that sort of advice would have been enough to deter me. Instead, what they said only served to strengthen my resolve. Very few of them had had any direct dealings with the police service. They always kept themselves to themselves and out of trouble. Their perceptions of the police were based on third-hand accounts or what they'd read in the media.

However, it was true that fewer than half a dozen black and minority ethnic (BAME) officers worked for Lancashire Constabulary at the time. But that also didn't put me off. Neither did my early recollections of the way the police had failed to deal with those racist thugs during my schooldays.

Marge pointed out that this role would test me and push me in new ways, but it would also provide the sort of satisfaction that only helping others can.

My parents were genuinely worried for me. Like most Asians of their generation, they knew little about the police service. Policing for them was all about dealing with 'bad' people. They were convinced I would suffer physically and psychologically. Their concerns, about my safety were based on my physical stature and my shy personality. There was also another reason for their concern. It was common knowledge that corruption was widespread within the police in Pakistan; taking bribes and using excessive force was common practice. They thought our police service was the same.

That's not to say that all our police officers here are 'knights in shining armour'. There have been many cases in our media about 'police brutality' and police corruption, but those kinds of issues aren't present to the extent they are in the Indian subcontinent.

I understood my parents' concerns and tried to reassure them as best as I could, but it is fair to say they remained anxious about my career choice. However, early in 1989, I decided to take the plunge and submitted my application form.

The recruitment process at the time started with an application form, followed by psychometric tests, including a written exercise, verbal and logical reasoning, and numeracy. A successful paper sift was followed by a physical test, in which candidates had to do thirty sit-ups and thirty press-ups in a minute each, execute a standing jump, and run a mile and a half in twelve minutes.

Although I considered myself reasonably fit, continuous running was never my thing, and I just about managed to complete the running test in eleven and a half minutes. The other elements of the physical test were less demanding.

A pass in the physical test was followed with a home visit by a local sergeant, who checked and confirmed my identity, checked that our finances were in order, and asked if we owned or rented our house. We had recently bought (in 1988), 44 Sandown Court, Avenham,

Preston, an apartment in a block of private apartments. One of the other questions he asked was whether we intended to get married. We of course said yes.

Haven't times changed? Can you imagine this question being asked today?

Following the home visit, I then endured two interviews. A competency-based interview conducted by HR, and then what was called a 'final' interview, conducted by an assistant chief constable (ACC). I remember the ACC grilling me about current affairs and asking me what my thoughts were on the student disturbances in China. Quite how my knowledge, or lack of it on this subject, was relevant to me becoming a competent police officer was beyond me. But I wasn't going to ask an ACC for an explanation. Getting through the nerve-racking interview was bad enough.

Everyone who joins the police service is vetted, which means checks are carried out on you, your partner or spouse, you children, and both sets of families if you're married or in a relationship. Following my vetting clearance and satisfactory references, an offer of 'probationary police constable' was made and gratefully accepted.

The police officer recruitment process is one of the lengthiest for any job; some applicants have had to wait up to two years for completion, especially those who've spent time abroad. Thankfully, after starting my recruitment process in March 1989, I was given a start date of 23 October 1989.

Despite my parents' early reservations, my father became quite proud of me, happily telling his friends that his son was a *poleeceman*.

Chapter 15

Surviving the Police Training Environment

I felt quite pleased with myself. I thought I'd done the hard bit by getting through the most rigorous recruitment process I'd ever undertaken. Unfortunately, it was only the beginning of the most stressful period of my life. Nothing in my sheltered and limited life had prepared me for the sixteen weeks I had to endure at the police national training centre.

I was part of the Lancashire October '89 intake sent to Bruche, in Warrington (closed several years ago following restructuring and budget cuts). Bruche was a regional training centre for police forces from Cheshire, Cleveland, Cumbria, Durham, Greater Manchester, Lancashire, Merseyside, Northumbria, the Midlands, and the Yorkshire forces.

Before I went to Bruche, my intake was given a two-week induction course, at our HQ in Hutton. The course provided basic insight into policing, our command structure, and the many departments within the constabulary. During these two weeks, I managed to keep my nerve. Luckily, I wasn't put on the spot to answer questions or volunteer for role plays too often. And being able to come home every night helped immensely.

I dreaded going to Bruche, where I'd been told we would only be allowed to come home at the weekend. I was thirty-three, with the confidence of a shy teenager, and I'd never stayed away from home before, apart from that week in London on my computer course.

Once there, we were split into classes made up of students from different forces. I don't recall anyone from Lancashire in my class, which added to my anxiety. I had to face all the things I'd shied away from in the past; there was no hiding place there. In the past I could walk out of a canteen or leave a room full of visitors and strangers without facing consequences. Here, I had to get involved in role plays and discussions and present aspects of legislation, share definitions, and respond to questions from the class. I hadn't picked up a book since leaving school, and you all know how good I was at school! It now felt as if I was back there, but with a huge spotlight on me. My insides were churning over like the drum of a washing machine.

There were many moments when I felt I couldn't carry on. I tortured myself, always thinking I'd get the simplest of things wrong, fail the course, and let everyone down yet again. The more these thoughts went round my head, the more I worried. The more I worried, the more stressed I became. The more stressed I became, the less I slept. It became an unbreakable cycle.

There was no let-up in the evenings either. Following tea, we were expected in the bar area, where we had to be seen to be socialising and were observed and marked by our instructors. I had always hated being under any kind of scrutiny, always disappearing into the background. In the past, it had been easy for me to become 'invisible' in social events and gatherings. Not here. You were marked down for not engaging with your colleagues.

Another thing I found difficult was marching. I was so bad that my classmates from the forces spent their lunch breaks helping me practice. They also had 'left/left' printed on the back of my sweatshirt, a constant reminder of getting my steps wrong. This may seem cruel, but it was in line with the banter that was part of the police culture.

Yet, amazingly, we won the 'best turned out', which included uniform inspection and marching. This took place on our last day, during the 'passing out' parade. I was strategically placed in the middle of the class, where any mistakes were less obvious to spot.

Of course, I couldn't share how I was feeling with anyone, for fear of being ridiculed and feeling stupid. Rightly or wrongly, I also decided against telling Marge. As loving as she was, I felt she would just tell me to pack up the job, saying, 'No job is worth putting yourself through such mental torture.' I could not let her and my parents down again. So, I persevered.

I'm sure Marge knew how badly I was struggling at Bruche, but she let me deal with it in my own way, patiently and discreetly providing me with the necessary support. It always cheered me up no end when, once a fortnight, she came to visit me. Her visits provided me with enough strength to keep going.

***

As trainees, we were asked to keep a regular record of our continuous development in a folder called Personal Development Programme (PDP). I felt some of the trainers were rather 'savvy' when it came to writing up our PDPs. They would ask us about how we thought we were developing, what we thought our development needs were, and how we thought we could address those; then they would word it slightly differently when writing up our PDPs.

As for showing potential for a probationary police officer, I honestly believe I was borderline. In many other organisations, I would have been shown the door.

Physical training was another area I struggled in. Most of our physical training was about self-defence techniques. I was never an aggressive person, and during those training sessions, I really came across as meek and mild. In fact, one of my peers who had seen me play football asked me how I could be so aggressive on a football pitch but be so mild in these training sessions. At the time, I was unable to provide an explanation and shrugged my shoulders.

Today, I know that it was my passion for football that drove me to play football so freely and with such commitment. But my passion for most other things was rather strangled by my fear of getting them wrong.

My already low self-esteem and confidence took a further hammering when, during one of these training sessions, a physical trainer described me sarcastically as someone who 'will do all right as long as he doesn't have to deal with any rough stuff'. Admittedly, he was built like a brick shithouse—sorry, brick outhouse—and anyone who didn't measure up to his way of doing things was a great big 'soft tart', to use his words.

In contrast, one of our intake instructors, Sgt Ion from Cumbria, showed a lot of patience with me. His manner reminded me of Mr Marrier, my physics teacher at school, and gained my trust.

During one of his lessons, on equality and diversity, I mentioned something about my culture. Picking upon what I'd said, Sgt Ion asked if I would be happy to talk for ten minutes or so about my culture, maybe answer some questions. I was very apprehensive but nevertheless agreed. He arranged it at the end of lessons the following day.

To my amazement and delight, the ten minutes turned into more than an hour and a half. For the first time, I discovered I was able to relate well to my peers and knew a lot more than I had realised about my culture and race. I also had a bit of a knack for being able to explain areas of diversity in a way the others were able to understand easily, making them feel comfortable enough to ask personal questions.

I'd never realised before then that I had such a skill. Unfortunately, it was to lay dormant for the next decade or so while I tried to come to terms with the rest of my probationary period and my role as an operational police officer.

I was always envious of my colleagues who were able to relax and enjoy training courses, making the most of opportunities to get away from the day-to-day operational duties and catch up with friends they had made. For me, attending courses remained a constant cause of anxiety and stress caused by worrying about getting things wrong and showing myself up.

Thankfully, our training came to an end, with the passing out parade, a pleasant enough affair. All officers were given passes for their families to attend and observe the special day. For the ceremony, Marge was accompanied by her father, Jack; as an ex-army man, he loved seeing police officers marching on the drill square. My only regret was that my two sons could not be present to see it all. I hadn't yet found a way for my estranged wife to allow them to spend some time with me.

Chapter 16

My Operational Years

I enjoyed a well-earned week's holiday, following my uncomfortable but learning experience at Bruche. Unlike most of my colleagues, who had planned a week abroad, Marge and I decided to have a few days on home turf. Ever since we'd gotten together, we'd struggled financially. But always, we enjoyed what we could afford and went for a weekend in the Lake District. We chose a bed and breakfast in Far Sawrey on the quieter side of Lake Windermere, away from the packed streets of Windermere and Bowness.

The short break was just the tonic we both needed, walking along the peaceful lanes, discovering where Beatrix Potter lived, and having tea with a remarkable lady of eighty-six called Mollie Green. Mollie had run a tea shop from her tiny cottage until the previous year and was still as bright as ever,—sharing many of her memories with us.

Feeling refreshed, it was time to go back to police HQ for further 'in-force' training. Lasting two weeks, this included familiarisation with force processes, procedures, and paperwork, as well as some role-plays and self-defence training. Whoopie!

When I joined Lancashire Constabulary, it had six operational divisions, with its headquarters in Hutton. Following restructuring, several additional subdivisions were added, before settling once again on the previous structure.

The six operational divisions were:

- A Division, known as 'Western'—with its divisional HQ in Blackpool, covering Blackpool, Lytham St Annes, and surrounding areas
- B Division, known as 'Northern'—with its divisional HQ in Lancaster, covering Lancaster, Morecombe, Fleetwood, and surrounding areas
- C Division, known as 'Southern'—with its divisional HQ in Chorley, covering Chorley and surrounding areas
- D Division, known as 'Central'—with its HQ in Preston, covering Preston Fulwood, Lea Longridge, and surrounding areas
- E Division, known as 'Eastern'—with its HQ in Blackburn, covering Blackburn, Accrington, and surrounding areas
- F Division, known as 'Pennine'—with its HQ in Burnley, covering Burnley, Colne, Nelson, Padiham and surrounding areas

Our headquarters in Hutton was also known as G Division. As well as meeting the demands of the operational divisions, it included several specialist departments—Dog Section, Mounted Branch, Major Incident Team, Drugs Unit, Surveillance Unit, Underwater Search Unit, Vehicle

Maintenance Unit, Estates Department, the force Training School, Finance, HR, the Vetting Unit and Clothing Stores. The chief officer team was also based there.

In its heyday, Lancashire Constabulary's training school offered a variety of courses attended by officers from all over the world.

Each operational division included Criminal Investigation Department (CID), uniform response teams, neighbourhood teams, support units, community support / diversity teams, school liaison teams, traffic or road safety units, and the local HR teams.

Currently, the constabulary has three operational divisions. It merged Western and Northern divisions, Central and Southern divisions, and Eastern and Pennine divisions, whilst several departments were relocated to headquarters, including a centralised communications department.

Attachment to the Divisional Training Unit

The two-week familiarisation course at HQ was followed by ten weeks of attachment to the training unit in Preston. Each division had its own training unit, with a sergeant and up to six tutor constables. The basic idea for the new recruits, while working with a tutor constable, was to get through several set competencies. You began by observing your 'tutor con' dealing with incidents; as you gained confidence, you dealt with the incidents while the tutor con observed your performance, progressing from basic incidents to more complicated ones. The tutor con provided feedback, highlighted areas for further development, and wrote up your progress in the PDP, which was an integral part of your two-year probationary period.

After being with my tutor con for several days, dealing with complaints of noise, parking issues, and generally giving directions and advice to members of the public, I made my first arrest.

We had been asked to attend a large store in the Fishergate Shopping centre, where we were met by a security guard. He outlined why he had detained a male in his early twenties. I then cautioned and arrested him, all very straight forward. My tutor con called for the police van to transport us back to Preston police station. Although the suspect was not violent, he was handcuffed as per guidelines, and taken to the van. As I placed him in the back of the van, he went in as far as he could and curled up into a ball.

Surprised, I asked him what he was doing.

'Aren't you going to give me a kicking? That's what I've had previously,' he said.

My tutor con and I looked at each other and shook our heads. I thought to myself, *surely this sort of thing didn't still happen ... did it?* I have to say I never witnessed any unnecessary use of force throughout my career with Lancashire Constabulary, although I was aware of numerous complaints of this nature against several officers.

Once I had completed and passed all the set competencies, within a ten-week period, I was declared fit for independent patrol and assigned to my first posting.

My first station

My assigned station was Fulwood, approximately a mile north of Preston city centre. It covered as far west as Blackbull Lane, all the way east to the M6 at Samlesbury, and north of Blackpool Road, to Bilsborough.

I was put on Team 2, part of four uniformed response teams. Each team had three vehicles at their disposal—two patrol cars and a van. The sergeant and the inspector were also provided with vehicles of their own, as was the small CID team.

All probationary officers went on to uniformed response or 'section' duties. As a response officer, you patrolled your allocated area in a marked police vehicle, usually on your own. As a probationary officer, you were either put in company with a more experienced officer or on foot patrol. While on patrol, you responded to jobs allocated to you or generated your own work, such as vehicle stop checks.

For my first few weeks, my sergeant put me in company with another officer. The sergeant was a pleasant and cheerful man. He was always very friendly and approachable though, like most officers, careful in what he said or how he behaved in my company. I sensed perhaps this was due to my background, but the whole team relaxed once they got to know me.

The officer assigned to me, PC Halibutt (not her real name) was also very bubbly and friendly. Previously she had worked as a tutor con and was very experienced in looking after the probationers. 'Probationer' is a term used for all police officers who are in their probationary period—usually the first two years of service. Sometimes this is extended if an officer requires further development.

While I was working with PC Halibutt, we were sent to deal with a man who wanted to make a complaint about juvenile nuisance outside his house, occurring regularly in the evenings.

When we arrived at the complainant's address, in my eagerness to show willing, I got to the front door first, followed by my colleague.

I knocked on the door and a large, angry man answered the door.

Before I could say anything, he, aggressively, shouted, 'I want to see a proper policeman, not one of you!'

I must admit I was flabbergasted and didn't know what to do and sheepishly looked to my more experienced colleague. PC Halibutt simply said, 'It's all right, Mebs. I'll deal with it.'

While I sat in the van, she took details of the incident and pacified him. At the time, I felt relieved, thanking my lucky stars she was with me. However, having now reflected upon it, I feel my colleague failed to address his blatant racist behaviour.

Back then, I didn't have the confidence to tackle my colleague or raise it with my sergeant. Unfortunately, behaviour of this nature was something I learned about from many of my black and Asian colleagues later in my service.

Team-bonding activities

Being a police officer is a thoroughly rewarding job; but can also bring a fair share of pressure and stress. Dealing daily with some members of the public can take its toll; you wind up dealing with a lot of people whose only contribution to society is to cause misery and pain to others or who, due to their addiction or dependence on alcohol, don't really care about anyone else.

To alleviate any stress and keep up morale, our team, like others, would go to the local pub after an early shift. Having gone along with these 'team-bonding' sessions for the first few times, I eventually started to make excuses and stopped going.

The times I went, I just watched or listened to others, chatting, drinking, and laughing. It seemed to release their work-related stress and frustrations. Those sessions did nothing for me. I was with my team, yet I felt alone and alienated from them, contributing little to any team bonding.

Over time, I slowly gained confidence and started to develop well as a police officer. I'd developed enough confidence to say to the team that we should look for other ways of team bonding and suggested we go tenpin bowling or play squash together. To my surprise, both suggestions were taken on board, with squash becoming a regular once-a-week event after our early shift.

At work, each shift began with 'parading on', a term used for when the team shares information on incidents since they were last on and when any outstanding jobs are allocated. There was a time when a team parading on for duty was lined up and inspected by the duty inspector for appearance and general tidiness before being allowed out on patrol. It has been known that some officers were sent home to get changed and smarten up before being allowed out on patrol. That practice stopped some years before I joined.

Police driving course

I'd been with my team for about three months and was competent enough to be dealing with most jobs on my own and gaining confidence all the time when my sergeant put me forward for my police driving course. That gave me a further sense of achievement and boosted my confidence.

The driving course, a two-week residential, took place at the constabulary's headquarters. Initially, I was gripped with apprehension, but gradually I began to relax and passed the course comfortably. Hardly surprising really when you consider I had been driving buses for nearly eight years! There were several driving manoeuvres to be completed, but the most uncomfortable aspect of the course was the 'running commentary' while driving and, of course, the classroom work. I was still apprehensive about those.

Due to how I was on the training courses, some of my colleagues may have thought me unsociable or unwilling to talk to them; nothing could have been further from the truth. I was simply too nervous and shy.

How do you like camping?

One of the constants in the police service was the frequent movement of police officers. We regularly had officers moving to different teams or leaving for different roles; some even changed forces, whilst a few left the police service altogether. Any shortfalls were filled with transferees or new recruits. One of the officers who joined my team was PC Darryl Shucks, who had transferred from Blackpool. He was an amazingly effective and dedicated officer but with enough shyness in his character to enable us to become friends. He was also an experienced hillwalker and Scoutmaster. Although Marge had ignited my passion for the countryside, it was Darryl who properly introduced me to hillwalking, taking me to the Lake District regularly and teaching me how to read maps and use a compass. Following several day trips, walking many of the smaller peaks around Ambleside, he asked, 'How do you like camping?'

I told him I'd never been camping, not even at school.

He was flabbergasted. 'Well, we'll have to put that right, won't we?'

he said with a smile on his face. We agreed to go camping on our next long weekend off.

I hadn't realised how much planning went into it camping. For me, it was a case of two friends meeting up, driving to the lakes, and off we went and set up camp before it got dark. Darryl came over to our house a few days before our camping trip to plan it all. He had brought some of his Ordnance Survey maps with him and several bits of 'kit' that he always took with him. As we sat down, I watched him plan and write down each leg of our walk, before writing out a second copy, which he said he always left with his wife, in case of any mishaps. He then went through all the kit we would need with me and how to pack it all.

Early on Friday morning, Marge agreed to drop us off at our starting point by the side of Wast Water in the Wasdale valley and then to pick us up on the Monday—giving us three nights' camping experience. We set off on a bright sunny day, with blue sky as far as you could see. It was the sort of day when you longed to be in the countryside.

As we skirted along the eastern shore of the lake at the bottom of the slope leading up to Scafell Pike, I found the going tough. Although I'd kept myself fit, the wet, slippery rocks and scree tested a different set of muscles and made progress slow. We soon fell behind our planned times. The climb up to Scafell was no picnic either; I had to ask Darryl several times to stop and let me catch up. As we approached the upper slopes, the weather closed in, and the clouds and rain very quickly engulfed us. It was time for our waterproofs. Visibility was down to about three or four yards. I was relieved when we reached the summit, thinking we could rest a while, have a hot drink, and get my breath back.

Oh no. Darryl told me, due to the conditions, it was best to get off the mountain as quickly as possible.

I must admit, at that precise moment, the mountain and the countryside had lost their appeal. I must have had pain and discomfort etched on my face, as Darryl asked if I was all right. I wanted to say, 'Terrific,' but just made some unintelligible groaning noise.

When we got to the bottom, it was still light, and Darryl suggested we set up camp before it got dark. We then sat down to what was my first ever meal in the great outdoors—a soggy tuna sandwich.

It rained all night, with the wind growing into a gale force; every gust of wind flattened our tent. Neither of us got much sleep that night. The next morning, the wind had died down. After making a strong cup of tea, we sat down to enjoy it; because of little sleep the previous night, we were both so tired, as we sat down, we both fell asleep. By the time we woke up, about an hour or so later, the tea had completely gone cold.

I enjoyed the walking over the next two days and saw some stunning views, but I must admit, I was awfully glad to see Marge waiting for us to bring us back home.

Community beats: Good old-fashioned policing!

Community policing has been introduced and reintroduced time and time again in the police service. The local 'beat bobby' walks around his or her patch, providing a reassuring presence; talks to the residents, telling youngsters off for some minor misdemeanour, taking part in local parish meetings, setting up neighbourhood watch schemes, and encouraging people to attend housing association meetings; and has a brew with the school governors, councillors, and members of the local community. From my experience, the public loved this way of policing and would often complain of how they missed not seeing an officer walking around their area. However, for some forces, this style of policing was seen as a bit of a luxury, to do 'if possible' after ensuring other priority areas of policing had been adequately resourced.

Many rank-and-file officers were not keen on it either; it was just not 'sexy' enough for them. Operational officers got more of a buzz from car chases, with adrenaline rushing through their veins. Community policing was seen as the 'pink and fluffy' aspect of policing. They preferred response or an opportunity to work in a specialist department such as CID. Added to this, some senior officers were more worried about how their crime figures would look to the Home Office than the public wanting to see their local officer walking on their beat.

This was re-enforced by whenever there was any shortage of officers on response, as officers from community policing were the first to be deployed onto these roles—or wherever there was a shortfall, often as a result of the sergeants failing to plan ahead.

I'd settled down well in Team 2 and began to enjoy being part of the team and hadn't thought of moving to another role. However, my sergeant called me into his office one day and brought out a letter he had recently received. The letter was from a lady, full of kind words about the way I had dealt with her teenage son and the level of empathy I had shown. He suffered from a mild form of depression and often vented his frustrations by causing minor damage to an empty property nearby. At the same time, my sergeant had also been asked to nominate an officer from his team for the new community beats initiative. Based on that letter, he thought I would be ideal for the role and put me forward.

In April 1991, I joined the community support team, under the supervision of Sergeant Ray Furness. Sgt Furness was particularly good to me and was one of those rare officers who always backed his team and fought in their corner. The team had eight constables working in two teams covering seven different beats that made up the Fulwood area. Due to the amount of work on the Moor Nook beat, it was allocated two officers.

One of the officers, PC Roger Turp, had been on his beat, Fulwood West, before this new initiative was set up. Some say he had been given his beat by Sir Robert Peel himself—not true. Roger was on his beat even before Sir Robert!

I worked closely with PC Kay McGovern, who had the adjoining beat (Brookfield).

***

The two teams worked the two different shift patterns, so each team could cover for the other team, with alternative weekends off. Operations, usually in plain clothes, were often mounted following a spike in crimes, such as auto theft, house burglaries, public order offences, or juvenile nuisance incidents and so on.

The beat work had its compensations. We had more weekends off than the response teams, the latest we worked was until midnight, unless there was a planned operation, and we had more freedom to plan holidays with our families.

There was always banter between beat officers and our response colleagues, often taking the mickey out of each other. We saw them as adrenaline junkies, feeding off the thrills of car chases and locking people up. We often felt they never understood or appreciated our role, which they saw as just having cups of tea with dear old ladies. But of course, to us, our role was all about working with others to find long-term solutions to crime. (Sounds a little defensive, doesn't it?)

This banter also extended to other departments and between police officers and police staff. Interdepartmental banter was much more apparent between uniform and CID officers, who saw themselves as the elite of the police service and could often be condescending towards officers in uniform. In my view, worst of all was the attitude of most police officers towards 'specials'. These were officers who did the same job as regular officers but without pay, as volunteers. They were often given the most menial of tasks and left guarding crime scenes.

'Assistance required'

I am the first to criticise the police service for getting things wrong; however, there is one thing that works incredibly well in the police service. No matter what the circumstances, irrespective of any rivalry, nothing stops an officer rushing to the aid of a colleague.

A shout for 'assistance' is responded to by every officer, regardless of what he or she may be doing. When it's heard, all banter, rivalries, and disagreement are forgotten, as an unwritten code of practice is strictly adhered to by every officer.

I have both relied upon and followed this code on many occasions. One example is when I was on my 'patch' and had stopped a vehicle that had been reported as driving erratically around the community centre on Grange Avenue. As I was speaking to the driver, the occupants became aggressive. One by one, they got out of the vehicle and surrounded me. I knew I was in imminent danger but kept my wits about me and quickly shouted into my radio, 'Assistance required, Grange Avenue.'

First, a lone patrol car came screeching towards me; it must have been nearby. Then within minutes, several other patrols appeared from nowhere. You cannot imagine how relieved I was to see so many of my colleagues come to my aid so quickly.

There's no doubt that immediate responses to such calls have saved many an officer from serious injury and even death.

As for the occupants of the car, they were all wanted with several outstanding warrants for their arrests and were promptly taken into custody.

'Mebs, they're here. Come and pick them up, love.'

The work I did as a community beat officer taught me a lot. Some of the first things I learned to do was to make myself known to the local residents and build close relationships with them. Close relationships were also built with the local councillors and businesses; with teachers and staff at Grange Primary School; and with the staff of the local housing office, who were particularly friendly and supportive. There was always a brew ready and waiting whenever I walked through the door—just what was needed on a wet and cold day.

There are often many negative stories in the media about some residents of council estates, which can lead to stereotypical perceptions of all residents of these estates. In my experience, these are often exaggerated; many decent people live on these estates. One of my fondest memories involves one such resident. She was a mother of two well-known drug addicts. They both had a series drug habit and several convictions for breaking into cars, burglaries, and assault.

Their mother would often see me walking round the estate, eventually approaching me for a chat. I was initially a little cautious, but she was friendly and easy to talk to. Her home soon became one of my first brew stops. She would openly talk about her sons, wishing there was something she could do to help them. But after she'd lost her husband, she said they'd both lost their way. The lady also knew all the comings and goings on the estate. If a new car or a stranger came onto the estate, she would know about it. She would have made an ideal neighbourhood watch coordinator, but because of her sons, that was not an option I could explore.

It's what she did on a regular basis that initially shocked the communication operators at Fulwood police station. The first time she rang the station and asked them to pass an urgent message to me, the operator did not take her seriously.

The operator radioed me and said, 'Mebs you're not going to believe this, but there is a lady on the phone asking me to pass a message to you. She says you'll understand. The message is, 'They're both here; come and pick them up, love.'

I knew exactly what she meant. I told the operator I'd explain later but to send the van to the lady's home address, as I was on my way there. I got to her home just as the van was pulling into her street.

As I brought her two sons out to the van, the two surprised officers asked me, 'How did you know they'd be here?'

I just looked at them and said smugly, 'All down to good old community policing, lads,' and winked at the mother.

The lady would 'shop' her sons to me without hesitation every time they came home. She hoped that, perhaps, doing time may help them overcome their addiction. Unfortunately, that was not to be, but she nevertheless continued to shop them.

A further point worth making about working on these two council estates is that, throughout my time there, I never came across any form of racism towards me. I'm not saying there was no racism on the estates, just that I did not face any from the residents there. I began to realise this was partly due to my personality, my attitude, my approach to people, and the non-judgemental way I dealt with them. It all helped me to relate to them.

I have always tried to treat people with respect, which has served me well. It's something I inherited from my father. I was also beginning to realise that perhaps I did have something positive to contribute to others and to the wider society.

I was slowly beginning to like my role. Dare I say it? I was beginning to enjoy it.

'Blackburn is full of Pakis'

My next operational memory is from the 1990s, when I was part of a police unit sent to Blackburn to deal with rising tensions between the Indian and Pakistani communities. It had started out as a 'boy meets girl' incident, to which both families took exception, and all sorts of gossips spread among both communities. It blew up into a major public order situation, with a small number of buildings being set alight by Asian youths.

Blackburn had one of the highest populations of British Asians in the country, with the textile industry attracting many first-generation immigrants to the area. With this and other industries in decline, Blackburn's unemployment and poverty levels rose to among the highest in the country. Despite its many challenges, including a prominent base for the National Party in the 1970s, surprisingly, Blackburn hasn't seen major riots, like those in neighbouring Burnley and Oldham.

However, as tensions between the two communities began to escalate, Eastern Division requested support from neighbouring divisions, who responded by sending as many officers as they could spare to Blackburn, including my own Central division.

But I was not in one of the first batch of officers deployed there. By the time I was sent, the situation had calmed down considerably. All the same, we were asked to make our way to the central police station, on North Gate, in case it all kicked off again.

We parked outside the old police station and stayed in the vehicle while the sergeant went inside for deployment instructions. Our unit was made up of six constables, all with riot gear at the ready. We'd been waiting for about half an hour, fidgeting, bored, and wanting to know what was happening, when suddenly one of my colleagues, Jon (not his real name) blurted out, 'Blackburn is full of Pakis.'

We were all shocked, not believing what we'd just heard. Then, as I was the only Asian officer there, they all looked at me expectantly, clearly thinking it was my responsibility to deal with Jon's comments. Momentarily, I looked back at them, to see what they would do but also to buy myself some time to figure out what to do next.

Finally, I simply said, 'What do you mean by that, Jon?'

Jon slowly turned to me, his eyes flickering rapidly, finding it difficult to maintain eye contact, as the wheels of his mind tried to catch up with what he had just uttered. He was already turning red from the neck upwards. 'I'm sorry. I'm sorry,' he said quickly. 'I didn't mean that. I didn't mean how that came out.'

Looking him straight in the eye and not flinching at all, I asked, 'What do you mean?'

He struggled to make a meaningful response or get any more words out, as his embarrassment took over. The panic in his eyes was becoming obvious to us all.

Nothing further was said as Jon, drowning in sheer panic, failed to explain himself. We waited for the sergeant to return in silence. It was another fifteen minutes before he came back to the carrier. Nobody mentioned anything to him. The sergeant simply told us we were standing down and making our way back to Preston to resume our normal duties.

The banter that took place on our outward journey had completely disappeared on the return journey. If the sergeant picked up on the change in the atmosphere, he never said. Once in Preston, Jon; another colleague, Terry (not his real name); and I made our way back to Fulwood. No one spoke for the whole journey. I'd known Jon for several years and would not have put him down as a racist. He'd spent time building relationships with people from different backgrounds and was very tolerant of people from all backgrounds.

What I decided to do next may not be what others in my situation would have done. Upon our return to Fulwood Police Station, instead of dealing with this incident formally by submitting a report for the incident to be investigated, I approached Terry, and together we hatched a plan to teach Jon a lesson he would never forget.

A few minutes later, I had briefed the duty inspector, Dave Asbridge, of my plan. It's fair to say that, in today's politically correct climate, a duty inspector would simply not go along with such a plan, but Dave agreed. I then went into the parade room, where Jon was doing some paperwork. He was about to apologise, but abruptly, I cut him short. I told him I had reported the incident to the duty inspector, who now wanted to see him. He started to shake as he got up to make his way to the inspector's office on the first floor. He had a petrified look on his face, and as we say in the police service, he was 'bricking it'.

Jon walked into the inspector's office; Terry and I discreetly followed him and stood outside the office. Dave told Jon a formal complaint had been made against him and asked him to explain his comments. We then heard Jon's feeble attempts to explain himself. We desperately tried not to laugh. Following his interrogation by the inspector, both Terry and I were called in. We saw Jon stood in front of the inspector, head bowed, looking sheepish. The inspector turned to us and said, 'I have heard what this officer has to say. Is there anything else the two of you want to add before I submit this as a formal complaint? Of course, this means Jon will most certainly lose his job.'

Jon now began to tremble and was struggling to maintain control. The two of us and the inspector looked at each other, trying to maintain our composure but simultaneously burst out laughing. After realising he'd been well and truly done like a kipper, Jon chased us out of the inspector's office, cursing as he did so.

I had decided to take this course of action, which some may see as making light of an immensely serious issue. I knew Jon; he wasn't a racist. In my view, he had made a genuine mistake. It was a slip of the tongue. But he wasn't going to get away with it scot-free. We had a lengthy and serious discussion about his outburst and the damage such a remark could cause to the organisation and to his BAME colleagues and the wider communities we served.

This was not an attempt to cover up a racist incident. I believed that, by getting the officer to understand his behaviour, I would prevent him from doing it again. I felt making a formal complaint would have either driven such comments underground or increased tensions between colleagues of different backgrounds or both.

Other people may have taken a different approach. My decision was made on what I thought was the right thing to do at the time. A formal complaint would probably have had dire consequences for Jon. But would it have changed his behaviour in the future? I don't believe it would have.

'Sorry, Mebs. I didn't know it was you.'

Another memory from days on my beat concerns one of my very few collaborations with colleagues from our CID team. Unfortunately, that experience only served to re-enforce many uniformed officers' perception of CID officers—that of smart suits, inflated egos, and a less-than-flattering attitude towards their uniformed colleagues.

Two officers from the CID team eventually turned to me for support after failing to find and apprehend a well-known burglar, Jason (not his real name). They'd been struggling to nab Jason for a while. I knew Jason well, and even though he was a rascal, I'd arrested him on several occasions and had a good relationship with him. I never looked down on him or judged him. There were lots of young men like Jason on my beat—the two brothers I've already spoken about and others—who had ended up trapped by the combination of poverty and drug addiction.

I knew Jason would always 'leg it', usually through the back door as soon as he heard a knock on the family's front door. When the two CID officers asked for my help, I advised them to wait until I'd gone to the back of the house before they knocked on the front door. Basic stuff, you would have thought. But for some reason they decided to ignore the advice of a mere PC plod.

By the time I managed to get to the back alley, about thirty metres away from the back of Jason's house, he was already coming out of the house and about to run off. Once Jason set off running, he was like a whippet; there was no catching him. Having got no reply at the front door, my two colleagues came running to the back alley, just as I shouted to Jason.

'Jason, stop. It's me, Mebs.'

To my colleagues' amazement, Jason stopped, came back to the three of us, and simply said, 'Sorry, Mebs. I didn't know you were after me. I only saw these two.' He pointed to my colleagues.

Their faces were a picture—mouths open but speechless.

One of them finally said, 'Well, I never. In all these years, I've never seen that before.'

With that, we put Jason in the back of their car and took him to Preston Police Station, where they, surprisingly, asked me to interview him. That was also a first for me—CID officers asking a beat officer to interview on their behalf. During the interview, Jason not only confessed to what he was arrested for but also to at least half a dozen other burglaries.

Not bad for a community beat officer.

'Say nothing; he's a copper!'

Year on year, Preston, like other cities and towns across the country, had seen a rising trend in the number of public order incidents in the city centre at the weekends. Many young people, having consumed too much alcohol, urinated publicly, fought each other, or turned on law-abiding citizens out with family and friends.

As such incidents escalated, my division responded with special operations on Friday and Saturday nights and a scaled-down version for Sunday nights. 'Operation Reassurance', as it was called, was to maintain presence in the city centre to reassure law-abiding members of the public and deter those looking for trouble. This usually meant Preston city centre was flooded with extra officers, wearing high visibility jackets, and patrolling around the town centre pubs, clubs, and food outlets—hotspots for such incidents, especially around closing times. Officers from community beats, traffic, and even CID, were drafted in for the weekend operation, providing plenty of overtime. We worked either 6 p.m. to 2 a.m. or 8 p.m. to 4 a.m. Friday through to Sunday. The operation lasted for several weeks, with all weekends and leave cancelled.

With so much activity during these shifts, it was never dull or boring. We were always called upon to deal with fights, customers refusing to pay, or colleagues shouting for 'assistance'. This was always worse when Preston North End played at home, with drunken fans from both sides squaring up to each other. Our role was to deal firmly with any public order incidents, arrest, and process culprits, and get back out as quickly as possible.

It was on one Friday night when a radio transmission caught my attention. I only heard the tail end of it, something like, 'A lad called Simon has fallen and has been taken to hospital by ambulance.' Straight away, I thought of our Simon. I knew he was often out with his mates at the weekend.

After speaking to the sergeant and with his permission, I headed off to Royal Preston Hospital's A & E department. There, to my horror, I found Simon, with one of his friends, both the worse for wear, waiting to be seen. Simon was holding blood-splattered tissues to his forehead. I approached the two of them, and before I could say anything, his friend stood up, positioning himself between me and Simon. He was facing me but looking at Simon, barely managing to stand up, and slurring his words. He said, 'Say nothing Simon. He'll stitch you up. Bloody coppers, they're all like.'

I tried not to laugh, as did a couple of nurses in the waiting area. It took Simon several goes to convince his friend that I was his stepdad. Although Simon had also had a few, he tried very hard not to laugh at the sight of his friend trying to give him advice!

"You do not have to say anything, but …"

The penultimate memory from my operational days concerns none other than the one and only Marge herself.

Whenever I was on a late shift (2 pm to 10 pm), Marge would always drop me off and pick me up, so she could use car for errands or shopping.

One such shift was on a Monday after we had spent the weekend with our friends in the Lake District. We had joined them in their timeshare lodge to enjoy many of the facilities there, including a large heated indoor swimming pool. Before settling down for some tea, we all decided to go for a swim. That's when Marge discovered she hadn't packed her swimsuit. Luckily, she was able to hire one from the resort.

When we got home on the Monday morning, while Marge was unpacking, she realised she'd forgotten to return the swimsuit. I told her not to worry; we'd send it back the next day. She then dropped me off at work.

I'd had a busy shift, working with Kay. There had been ongoing issues of juvenile nuisance around a care home on my patch, and several vehicles had also been damaged in the area. After chasing our tail with these juveniles, we both came back to the station a little early to finish off some paperwork.

It was while doing our paperwork that I remembered the unreturned swimming costume, and a cunning and devious plan began to hatch. I explained to Kay what I had in mind, and she, reluctantly, agreed to help. I then designed and printed off what looked like an arrest warrant for theft, with Marge's description and details of the swimsuit.

Usually when Marge came to pick me up, she would wait in the car until I came out. I purposely didn't go out and waited for Marge to come into the station. After waiting for a good ten minutes or so, she eventually came in and rang the enquiry desk bell. Kay went to the enquiry desk, while I hid out of sight but within earshot.

Kay put on her most solemn and serious face to greet her.

Straight away, Marge asked, 'What's wrong? Is it Mebs? What's happened?'

Kay slowly began, 'Marge, it's not Mebs. He's fine. I don't know how to tell you this. This is about you.' She continued deliberately and slowly. 'I wish I didn't have to do this, but this is extremely serious. I have here a warrant for your arrest.'

She showed Marge what I'd printed off and read out Marge's description, along with the description of the swimming costume, its value, and where it had been stolen from. Marge had never seen a warrant before.

'What? You are kidding. Arrest me? You're not serious, are you?' Marge's voice began to break.

'I'm sure it's just a misunderstanding, and you'll be able to explain it all,' Kay went on. 'But tell me, have you been to a timeshare in the Lake District, and did you hire a swimming costume? Did you return it?'

'Oh my God, oh my God! Yes, yes, I forgot to return it, but it only happened at the weekend. Tell them I will return it," replied Marge, urgency and fear in her voice.

'I'm so sorry to tell you this Marge, but the owners have contacted Cumbria police, and they have issued this warrant for your arrest, I have no choice but to arrest you,' Kay told her with sympathy in her voice.

It was at this point that Marge's bottom lip started to quiver, as she'd never been in trouble with the police.

Poor Kay. The sight of Marge about to break down got to her, and she could no longer maintain her composure. But before she could say anything, I jumped in front of the enquiry desk shouting, 'Arrest her, arrest her!' laughing as I did so.

'He set me up, didn't he? Oh, the little …,' Marge said, wiping tears from her eyes. wait till I get him home!'

It was something she never lived down for weeks, especially when she came to pick me up. Marge never suspected anything and later told me she didn't think I was capable of anything like that.

What I did to Marge demonstrates the change I was going through following the years since we'd first met and after I'd become a police officer. I guess the change in me had managed to bring out a wicked sense of humour, hidden for far too long!

Bob and Dorothy Snape: An unforgettable couple

As already mentioned, Kay and I worked on adjoining beats, and we would often walk out to our beats together.

Mahmood Ahmed

One day on our way back to the police station, Kay took me to the home of a couple she knew and introduced me to Bob and Dorothy Snape.

Of all the people I have ever met, Bob and Dorothy were the kindest and most caring. Both devout Christians, they always went to church on a Sunday and yet never pushed their beliefs onto anyone; and they were quite at ease with my own Islamic faith.

Their natural manner, happiness, and zest for life was refreshing to see in a world that often smacks of insincerity and selfishness. Their willingness to help others, their friendliness towards strangers, and their uniqueness only helped re-enforce everything good about humanity. They were overjoyed every time Kay and I walked into their bungalow, treating us as family and welcoming us with open arms.

Sadly, Dorothy is no longer with us.

I want to take this opportunity to thank Bob and Dorothy for reminding me there are still such special people in the world.

Bob and Dorothy, I will always be grateful for your kindness.

Chapter 17

A New Opportunity, a New Challenge!

I'd been serving as a uniformed officer for ten years at my one and only station, Fulwood, when a new opportunity came knocking on my door. This opportunity was to take me in a completely different direction, away from front line policing and into an area I'd never considered before. It was an opportunity requiring a set of skills and expertise I didn't know I had.

The relationship between the police service and diverse communities has always been difficult and fractious, with trust and confidence on both sides low and continuing to erode. Numerous large-scale race riots in our inner cities, over several decades, highlighted the tensions the police service often tried to gloss over. This was a concern the Home Office was aware of, and its response was to implement half-hearted new initiatives—in an effort to demonstrate the desire to change things.

One of these initiatives was to increase black and minority ethnic (BAME) representation within the police service, the lack of which the Home Office had been aware of since 1971. The figure then was abysmal, just 0.043 per cent of total police strength. Despite this and a further report commissioned by the Home Office in 1979, little changed as a result.

It took two further inquiry reports—published almost two decades apart—for the Home Office and the police service to take what some considered to be seriously long-overdue action.

Following the disturbances in London in 1981, the first of these two reports was published by Lord Scarman. This report encouraged the police service to put more emphasis on efforts to engage with diverse communities. However, some saw those recommendations as nothing more than token gestures, making no actual difference to the relationship between the police and the BAME communities.

A second report followed an inquiry by Lord Macpherson in 1999 into the Metropolitan Police (Met) investigation of the tragic murder of a black teenager, Stephen Lawrence, in 1993. This inquiry went much further than the Scarman report. It highlighted the Met's failings, making more than seventy recommendations and, controversially, labelled the police service as 'institutionally racist'.

Even before the Macpherson report, chief officers agreed work was needed for their forces to be reflective of the communities they served. However, not all had given it the credence it needed, some failing to see it required careful policy development, implementation, and monitoring. Following the report, forces acknowledged the level of work needed, but many refused to accept that they were 'institutionally racist'.

Also, in the late 1990s, the ruling Labour government had recognised that the political climate had shifted considerably. The recommendations made by Lord Macpherson were welcomed by the then home secretary, Jack Straw. In 1999, he announced his ten-year employment targets for all police forces. These targets would require each force to submit current officer data broken down by ethnicity and rank and report on what interventions were being put in place to meet his targets. Later, these targets were to include police staff and special constables.

The response from some forces could, at best, only be described as lukewarm. A few even blamed the lack of representation on BAME communities, claiming they showed no interest in joining the police service. On the other hand, many within BAME communities felt the targets didn't go far enough, and there were no sanctions for failing forces—without sanctions, failing forces had nothing to worry about.

Here in Lancashire, there appeared to be some genuine desire to address this situation, even if the constabulary was pushed into it by Mr Straw's targets. It led to a rethink about how the constabulary was going to attract, recruit, and progress BAME staff.

The force's 'enthusiastic' response was given further impetus by pressure from community leaders, lobbying groups, and activists. The most notable of these were the late Lord Adam Patel and my old friend Ibby, Ibrahim Master, who had both been pushing for greater effort from the force for many years prior to the targets. Ibby was a member of the Lancashire Police Authority and later became the deputy police and crime commissioner for Lancashire, challenging and holding the constabulary to account on many areas of policing.

On a personal level, Ibby was very generous with his time for me, providing the use of his home for some of the meetings and freely offering much-needed advice.

This led to the force agreeing to create a new post. The post, based within the HR recruitment team at HQ, would lead on this piece of work. That post was for a 'minority ethnic communities liaison officer' (MECLO). MECLO would lead on all aspects of workforce representation, developing and implementing initiatives to promote career opportunities within Lancashire Constabulary to the BAME communities. The role holder would engage with BAME communities; help build relationships, trust, and confidence; and encourage people from BAME communities to consider careers with Lancashire Constabulary, providing support and guidance throughout the recruitment process.

BAME communities' representatives, the chief officer team, and the recruitment manager all agreed it had to be an officer from the BAME background—their rationale being it had to be someone who understood the diversity of cultures and the complex make-up of those communities, who would be aware of the suspicions and reservations they had, and who would be able to help them overcome the many challenges they faced when wishing to apply. Such knowledge and skills would make it easier for the officer to relate to the BAME communities, whilst also acting as a role model and a conduit.

This was an opportunity made for me. Following my expression of interest, I was invited to an interview, along with several other candidates, including those from the sergeant and inspector ranks. The interview was conducted by the recruitment and selection manager, Thelma Aye, supported by an HR colleague and a senior officer.

Thelma, providing feedback after the interview, said that, although there were several good candidates, it was my passion for the role that impressed her the most. It was the first time I'd ever been able to openly demonstrate my passion for anything other than football and Marge of course.

Late in 1999, I left my operational role at Fulwood and took up my new post at the force headquarters. I was so pleased and proud to have beaten officers of higher ranks to the role and have gotten it on merit. I'd never learned the art of 'using who you know'; nor did I want to.

However, this 'strategy' had been a major part of appointments within the police service. Yet white staff—mainly white male staff—feel that minority staff, including females, get preferential treatment when applying for certain roles because of their background. My view is that there may have been such cases, but they are dwarfed by those who have been given certain roles because of who they knew or the 'old boys' network' as it is known. It is something the police service and the Home Office have never been able to address or change. Some feel they've never really tried.

I came across many who were totally unsuitable and incompetent in their roles but were there because of who they knew or someone 'looking after them'. It's common practice for many officers to build teams around them with people who look and behave like them and select those they know—unconscious bias in practice, some may say. Others would call it a very deliberate act.

Anyway, back to my new role and to put into context how big a task I was facing, many of my colleagues at Fulwood shared with me how they felt about it. Almost all disagreed with what the force was doing; they felt the force was kowtowing to the demands of the government and minority groups, disagreeing with the need for targets altogether. Although they were small in numbers, they probably reflected thoughts of many white officers across the force.

Despite some resistance, including from some senior officers and the trade unions, Lancashire Constabulary went ahead with the role in its desire to address under-representation within the force.

Mahmood Ahmed

Putting the foundations in place

Throughout my life people have told me, 'Where there's a will, there's a way.' I now had the will and was determined to find a way. I was blessed with supervision who believed in me and the work we were doing—none more so than the incredibly unselfish Thelma Aye, my immediate supervisor.

Thelma had joined the constabulary perhaps two or three years before I took up my new role. Having previously worked in the private sector, Thelma was a breath of fresh air, liberating her staff from the chains of micromanagement, prevalent within the police service. She was an 'enabler', encouraging her staff to think for themselves and outside the usual box and never taking credit for her staff's good work. She gave credit where it was due and often praised her staff in the presence of senior officers, a rarity within the police service, thus boosting staff morale and confidence.

My passion for the role was matched by my desire to help people, to build bridges, and to create a better understanding of BAME communities and of the police. I had hoped, by taking these steps, I could help build trust and confidence and increase BAME interest in joining the police.

Lancashire had a sizeable BAME community, spread across central and eastern parts of the county. Preston was the most diverse, with a large black and Asian community. East Lancashire had some of the highest Asian populations anywhere in the country.

It was mainly these areas of the county where my focus lay. Although they kept their distance, the older generations from BAME communities were respectful of the police. In contrast, the younger generations had a rather different perspective. Whereas the older generation had little or no interaction with the police—if wronged, they simply took it on the chin and carried on—this was not so with the younger generation. They didn't feel their chins were there merely as punchbags for the police. They were frustrated and angry, taking to the streets to let everyone know how they felt about being discriminated against and their unfair treatment by the police.

This became abundantly clear right from the start in my dealings with the BAME youth. I visited many BAME community centres and youth clubs to try to engage with them. Initially, many held strong hatred and resentment towards me, and they did not hold back. Many told me to, 'F – – – off.' They did not want to know anyone who worked for such a 'racist organisation' and asked if I was proud to have 'sold out'. Some called me a 'coconut'—a term for someone who is brown or black on the outside and white on the inside, basically a black or brown person who behaves and thinks like a white person.

Their anger was largely due to their experience of the police, especially among those who had been stopped and searched. Home Office data highlighted the disparity in stop-and-search going back over several decades. Disparities continued throughout the criminal justice system—including in number of arrests following stop-and-search, in prosecutions, and in the custodial sentencing handed out to those from the BAME background. Their anger and frustrations were understandable.

Despite what they thought of me and some rather uncomfortable conversations in the beginning, I understood where they were coming from. I increased my efforts to engage with them, with visits to community, youth, and religious centres becoming much more frequent.

I followed up the visits with radio interviews. I wrote articles for BAME newspapers and for a local magazine for the black community. I sent out invitations for them to attend meetings and focus groups, welcoming their views and experiences.

At the start, only one or two turned up. But slowly, the numbers increased. Meetings and focus groups provided a platform for their anger and a regular opportunity to get things off their chest. Gradually, I was able to get them to shift their focus from anger and resentment to contributing to bringing about change. With their stance slowly shifting, most agreed that 'having nothing to do with the police' was not an option. From these difficult beginnings, I was able to get closer to the BAME youth, the wider BAME communities, and some key influencers. The process of slowly earning respect and trust was beginning to take shape, allowing me to build meaningful relationships with our BAME communities across Lancashire.

Their views about me and the police became my tools for engagement to raise their understanding of the police and generate their interest. Admittedly, it was a slow process. It was never going to be anything else, following years of suspicion and mistrust.

From these meeting and focus groups, it was clear that some within BAME communities felt that 'positive action' initiatives didn't go far enough. They wanted 'positive discrimination' or at least 'affirmative action' initiatives, similar to those in America and Northern Ireland. However, every force in the country was against positive discrimination and affirmative action initiatives, as was I at the time. With almost every force failing to meet the targets—several by some distance, the government also lost its appetite, so much so the targets were withdrawn before the ten-year period. They were replaced with an ambiguous statement that 'forces must do everything they can to reflect the communities they serve'.

As I now look back, I feel we were too quick to dismiss the 'affirmative action' option. Well-thought-through affirmative action initiatives, alongside positive action initiatives should have been given greater consideration. Unfortunately, the government lacked the political will, and the police service lacked any genuine desire to tackle workforce under-representation. However, I could not say this was the case in Lancashire.

***

In 1999, Lancashire Constabulary's BAME officers made up less than 1 per cent of its workforce (six officers in total). This made meeting our employment target, year on year, an immensely challenging. However, Thelma and I set about it with great energy and vigour, ignoring the negativity around us.

In the next three years, I helped put together the Constabulary's Recruitment, Retention, and Progression strategy (RRP) within its Community and Race Relations Strategy (CRR). Putting together the CRR strategy was the work of many people—senior police officers, police authority members, the head of HR, and the head of learning and development, along with those from outside the force, such as key BAME community representatives and members of the independent advisory groups (IAGs). This included people like Ibby Master and Charu Ainscough, chair of the Strategic Independent Advisory Group. Both were tireless in their efforts to improve the working conditions for BAME staff and in supporting the constabulary to deliver an equitable service to all communities. Charu, like Ibby, gave me her valuable time and support freely. I am indebted to both for all their endeavours and their personal advice and guidance.

There is one other person to whom I will always be grateful—an HR manager at Eastern Division, Ann-Marie Bull. Her help to put together initiatives specifically designed for her division was immense. Eastern Division was chosen for a pilot scheme, as it had the largest BAME population and because of Ann-Marie's commitment and drive for the project. We very quickly developed mutual respect. It was obvious to me that she genuinely wanted to learn about people different to her, their ways, and their culture and to do something about under-representation. We became good friends and a valuable source of support for each other during our time with Lancashire Constabulary. This is the same lady who shared her dream with me, providing much needed inspiration for this book.

***

Once the RRP strategy was drawn up, I set about developing and implementing the following initiatives:

Review of the recruitment process and criteria

When I shared my thoughts on the then recruitment process with Thelma, she applied her ability to think outside the box. She employed the services of an occupational psychologist who, with my help, put forward several recommendations. These included diversity and unconscious bias training for the recruitment and selection team, those involved in paper-sifting application forms, and those involved in interviews and assessment centres. The need for a full driving licence was also removed, as it disadvantaged some female Asian applicants who, due to cultural reasons, were not encouraged to learn to drive.

Engagement initiatives

The way we engaged with our diverse communities was also reviewed. At the time, engagement was ad hoc and inconsistent, giving the impression that we only engaged with our BAME communities when things went wrong. To remedy this, I set up the following engagement initiatives:

- *Open or information days for BAME communities.* These were held on a regular basis within BAME communities, often taking advantage of community events such as the Caribbean Carnival, local melas, Diwali, Eid, and many other religious events. I attended these events with my police recruitment stand and information leaflets, supported by my colleagues from our specialist departments and local officers who were familiar with their community. The objective was to provide opportunities for people to learn about the police service, our recruitment processes, and the support available. Sometimes, often at the potential recruits and BAME communities request, the information sessions were held in several local police stations.
- *Careers fairs.* I attended careers fairs at several schools and colleges with high numbers of BAME pupils, while also focusing my attention on our universities—University of Central Lancashire (UCLAN), Lancaster University, and Edge Hill University. I built relationships with many student societies, delivering presentations and talks on wide-ranging policing topics and not

shying away from difficult issues like racism. There were other careers events and fairs too held at some of the local football clubs, which proved rich pickings for our recruitment campaigns.

- *Sporting events.* One of the simplest ways to bring people together was through sport. Football, cricket, and badminton were the three most popular. Matches between the local BAME communities and officers from their division were organised across Lancashire. These matches and tournaments were followed up by some food, at either a community venue or at our police headquarters, creating ideal opportunities to disseminate information on careers within the police service. I also invited several BAME officers along to share their journeys and experiences, followed by Q&A sessions.

- *Female-only events.* Football and cricket attracted entirely male interest, but we wanted to target BAME females too. Their representation was a much bigger challenge. Engaging with BAME females, especially those from the Asian Muslim background, was difficult due to cultural barriers. Most parents didn't want their daughters to attend mixed events. Therefore, using our female officers and staff, we organised female-only fashion shows, henna painting, and arts and crafts events, based on what they told us would attract females from these communities. This initiative earned the constabulary huge respect from the Asian community.

I feel I must share with you one story that stands out from attending one of the careers fairs mentioned above. It took place soon after Sgt Jameel Murtza had been appointed as my new supervisor, following Thelma's departure. We were working at Turf Moor, home of Burnley Football Club.

Jameel and I had an unwritten rule that we would never allow anyone to walk past our stand without trying to engage them. This meant that, irrespective of a person's age, background, and interest (or lack thereof) in joining the police service, if we were free, we would make every effort to talk to him or her.

While Jameel was busy with some students, who were totally mesmerised by him, I noticed a young man in his early twenties doing his best to avoid making eye contact with me as he walked past our stand.

'Good morning. How are you?' I asked in a friendly and upbeat manner.

'I am well, thanks,' he replied, and tried to move on quickly.

'What sort of job are you looking for?' I continued, ignoring his discomfort.

'Actually, I'm not sure. I'm going to have a good look around today,' he said quietly.

'We have lots of different jobs in the police service. Have you ever thought about joining the police?' I continued.

Straight away, he said he would never do that. When I pressed him further, he hesitated and then reluctantly told me he'd once had a terrible experience with the police. I was curious and pushed him to tell me more. He said he'd been beaten up by the police for no reason. I asked if that was in Lancashire.

I was flabbergasted when he said it had taken place several years ago—in Pakistan! His experience of the police halfway across the world had tarred his perception of the police in this country so badly that he wanted nothing to do with us.

- *Marketing strategy.* There is a well-known saying that goes something like this: 'If it ain't broke, don't fix it.' The marketing strategy, until then, had been working very well for the police service. Whenever the force announced it was recruiting, it was flooded with applicants. The strategy was simple, inexpensive, and highly effective. However, almost all the applicants were white; just announcing we were recruiting was ineffective in reaching out to our BAME communities. Therefore, a different strategy was required.

  This was, again, where Thelma proved herself invaluable to Lancashire Constabulary. She asked me to set up several focus groups, both internally and externally. In the meantime, she also made use of an external marketing company, specialising in targeting 'hard-to-reach' groups.

  They produced leaflets, posters, and newspaper adverts, which were presented to the focus groups. Eventually, a theme called 'In-Law', with a clever use of the word 'law', was chosen by the groups. Each leaflet, poster and the advert had a picture of a black or an Asian face with different slogans—'Father-in-Law', 'Mother-in-Law', 'Son-in-Law', and 'Daughter-in-Law'. Or they featured a picture of different black and Asian members of staff with the slogan, 'You give up a lot to become a police officer, but your identity isn't one of them.'

  This strategy and the subsequent campaigns were hugely popular with the BAME community and earned the constabulary a national marketing award.

  Before each recruitment campaign, there were leaflet drops within BAME communities and at religious and youth centres;

posters were put up and adverts were placed. These were followed up with articles and BAME staff profiles in *Asian Image*, *Asian Leader*, and *New Harmony Magazine* (no longer in circulation). I also did several radio interviews and discussions on many of the BAME radio stations, with live phone-ins.

Advanced marketing like this informed BAME communities of any impending recruitment campaigns by the constabulary, enabling me to develop 'nurture lists' for all those who were interested in joining the police service.

- *Positive action initiatives.* Our focus on attracting potential BAME recruits through the above initiatives dramatically increased expressions of interest and applications.

The next challenge for us was to support the increasing numbers of applicants through the various stages of the recruitment process. Several positive action initiatives were introduced, including:

1. *Mentoring.* Each candidate had an opportunity to be assigned an existing police officer as his or her mentor.
2. *Familiarisation events.* All those who showed an interest in becoming a police officer were given detailed information on the recruitment process, with discussions on each stage of the process.
3. *Application form workshops.* Workshops included explanations, 'dos and don'ts', pitfalls; an emphasis on attention to detail; and discussions on how to answer the competency questions.
4. *Mock interviews and assessment centres.* Candidates received advice on how to prepare for interviews and carry out

research to learn more about the job; had opportunities to sit mock interviews; and were given information on what to expect at assessment centres.

5. *Mock physical tests.* This included workshops on general fitness and diet and opportunities to sit mock physical tests.

It's fair to say that these positive action initiatives caused unrest among white male candidates; however, what the force or the police service was doing was not illegal.

• *Raising awareness of internal staff.* To maximise the impact of our various initiatives, it was imperative that staff within our recruitment and selection team understood why we were putting these initiatives in place. They were the ones who would be taking initial calls and dealing with enquiries. We did not want them putting anyone off by using inappropriate language or providing inaccurate information.

Naturally, this didn't sit comfortably with all of them. Some, like others within the constabulary, felt that, if people from any background wanted to join the constabulary, they should simply apply like everybody else, and nobody should be given 'preferential treatment'.

A workshop was organised to explain the background to the employment targets, the challenges people from different backgrounds face, and what was being put in place to address those challenges.

Following the workshop, most but not all, understood and supported what we were trying to do.

Not all forces embraced the employment targets

Just before Thelma left to take up her new post with RBS, Lancashire Constabulary was being recognised for our good work, with several forces keen to visit and learn about our initiatives.

When I started in my new role, I'd assumed all forces across the country were as eager as Lancashire Constabulary to address under-representation. *Why wouldn't they be?* I asked myself. After all, the employment targets were for all forces. However, a telephone conversation I had with one counterpart from a much larger force proved differently.

The conversation went something like this:

PC Naheem (not his real name). Hi, Mebs. My name is Naheem. I'm calling from our HQ. I've just taken up this post, and I've been told about the good work Lancashire are doing. I was wondering if we could meet to discuss your work.

Me. Hi, Naheem. Congratulations on your post! I'd be more than happy to share our work with you. Why don't you come over to us? I can show you around and introduce you to my line manager and our recruitment team.

PC Ali. Ah … Is it possible for you to come to me?

Me. Yes, of course.

It was only when I was leaving his place of work, whilst we were in the car park, that Naheem told me his force would not allow him to visit me. In his opinion, they were 'just going through the motions', it was a 'tick box' exercise, and he was in place so his force could say they were trying to address the issue.

Later, in a different role, I learned that many forces had the same attitude to the employment targets.

Luckily for me, with the continued commitment from our deputy chief constable, Steve Finnigan, and Supt Walker, things were different in Lancashire. I also had the full support of Supt Andy Pratt, whose clarity about what was needed often resulted in clashes with other senior officers on this and many other equality and diversity issues—but he never wavered. The other thing that helped me was the steady increase in the number of BAME police officers being appointed, a clear demonstration of the success we were achieving.

This work led to the number of BAME police officers more than doubling in the very first year. The good work started with Thelma, continued with Sgt Murtza, and later kept flowing with a team of officers taking over from both Jameel and me as we moved on to different roles.

Thelma's departure

They say you can be a victim of your own success. So it was with Thelma. Thelma was a hugely supportive individual who genuinely cared for her staff and wanted to do all she could for them. However, I had no idea what the good work we were doing would lead to. The constabulary was certainly making progress, as our success received national recognition, with several national awards for both the constabulary and me. I believe this was the first award of its kind for the police service in 2000. Approximately a year later, our success led to Thelma being headhunted by the Royal Bank of Scotland (RBS). RBS wanted her to lead their equality and diversity work. It was an opportunity we both knew she could not turn down.

Following Thelma's departure, I began to think about who might take over from her. I must admit, my old sense of insecurity started to creep back into my thinking. And for a while, I started to worry. Thelma was replaced swiftly, but her replacement was nothing like Thelma, and I struggled to build any kind of meaningful relationship with her successor.

However, I didn't need to worry for long. In 2001, the constabulary also appointed someone who would act as my direct supervisor and someone who would share my workload. That someone was Sgt Jameel Murtza.

Sgt Murtza, or Jameel as he asked me to call him, was a fellow Pakistani who had joined Lancashire Constabulary as a transferee from the Metropolitan Police. He was a very assured officer. Oozing confidence, he was charming and had a great sense of humour and an all-round personality that made him extremely popular. Much more importantly for me, Jameel provided me with the same kind of freedom I'd enjoyed with Thelma. He was also very much hands-on, actively supporting me while managing upwards. Younger than me, he was much more of a role model to the young BAME recruits we were trying to reach.

His charm and confidence, always apparent, were never more so than when we attended some of the big events such as the Mega Mela at Wembley, London, or at the NEC in Birmingham, where he was like a magnet, pulling young people towards our police stand. This made both events hugely successful engagement events and generated a great deal of interest among the BAME young people.

Chapter 18

Headhunted, Me? Pull the Other One!

In 2001, Thelma had left, and Jameel was now my supervisor. We had also become close friends, and things were going well for us.

However, even after Thelma's departure, it never occurred to me to broaden my horizons or look elsewhere. Some may say I lacked ambition.

But this changed by the end of 2001, when the idea of leaving Lancashire Constabulary was planted in my head by Thelma, now the group diversity manager at RBS. Thelma contacted me and floated the idea of me working with her again and on a fresh challenge. She told me together we could reach even more people at the RBS. Initially, I was cautious, but the very thought of what I could perhaps do at a much bigger organisation began to excite me. Besides, I'd always enjoyed working with Thelma.

Thelma couldn't resist the attraction of making her mark in an organisation that employed more than a hundred thousand people across the country, compared with fewer than seven thousand at the constabulary and to put diversity at the core of her new employer's work ethic.

She made it clear she saw me as an integral part of a team she wanted to put together. This put me in a rather difficult position. The role I had with Lancashire Constabulary was safe and secure. I knew that, if I stopped enjoying it, I could always go back to being an operational officer. There was the police pension to consider and our house, supplied rent-free. On top of that, everyone advised me against the idea.

I'd never experienced what it was like to be wanted, especially by one of the biggest banks in Europe. Me, being headhunted? I had not even dreamt of such things. For the first time in my life, I felt a buzz, a tingling feeling that came with having an opportunity at such a large organisation. I was beginning to think maybe I could go further; maybe this was an opportunity to remove the psychological chains that had been around my ankles all my life.

I'd never taken a risk or a chance on anything in my life before. I weighed everything up, thought carefully about the advice from my colleagues, discussed it at length with Marge, and decided to take a chance.

Poor Jameel. One minute we were planning all the things we were going to do together; the next he was trying to convince me to stay. But he knew I wouldn't get another opportunity like this again and that I would relish working with Thelma again. He reluctantly stepped aside and gave me his blessing, and we parted as good friends.

At the end of 2001, I left Lancashire Constabulary after twelve years. I arranged a 'leaving do' in a restaurant in Manchester. Many of my colleagues, friends, and members of the community travelled nearly forty miles to say their farewells, giving me a fabulous send-off.

The event provided much-needed confirmation of how highly I was thought of by both my colleagues and members of the BAME community—something my father would have been proud of. As sad as I was to be leaving Lancashire Constabulary, their send-off gave me a real sense of pride.

The RBS Experience

My time with the RBS group, from start to finish, fell considerably short of what I had hoped for. Many, including my stepdaughter, said my decision to join the RBS was a mistake.

Talk about stepping out of your comfort zone. I felt as if I had stepped into another world, a corporate world that may as well have spoken another language. I hate to admit it, but I was unable to cope with the private sector, so different from the public sector I had worked in all my life. I was out of my depth.

Thelma was the group diversity manager; I and two others were appointed as diversity managers, each with our own portfolios. My portfolio was made up of age, race, and religion. I had to hit the ground running, with calls, emails, and enquiries coming from every direction—people seeking advice and support or those wanting me to check their policies, processes, or procedures.

Without any specific training, I was beginning to sink fast and realised I was way over my head.

The role I'd performed with Lancashire Constabulary was of little help. Furthermore, I was ill prepared for the politics and competitive ambition of some of those I was working with. After only a month of joining, I was beginning to regret my decision.

The truth is, as good as I was at leading the workforce agenda for Lancashire Constabulary, I didn't have the necessary training for equality and diversity needed to succeed in the cut-throat financial sector. I began to search for a way out.

As the daily trudge of going to work got worse, Jameel, my knight in shining armour, came to my rescue. We had kept in touch. I told him how things were with me at the RBS, and he shared the progress he was making at the constabulary. Knowing my situation, he asked if I would be interested in returning to the constabulary.

Would I be interested? Are you kidding? I jumped at the chance.

My further good fortune was that Supt Wendy Walker was still head of recruitment and training, and along with the then deputy chief constable (DCC), they told Jameel to get me back as soon as possible. I was later the told that the DCC was so excited about the prospect of my return that she wanted to announce it before the return process had even begun.

The constabulary reinstated me with all my previous service intact and treated my time away as a 'career break'.

However, my six months with RBS was not a total disaster. I was able to buy the police house I was living in with the special mortgage rate for staff, and there were opportunities to build relationships and contacts with several external consultancy firms. A few approached me with offers of work. Their much better remuneration packages were tempting, but with my confidence depleted, I decided against such offers and took the chance to rebuild my career and confidence back at Lancashire Constabulary.

Whether people felt sorry for me or held me in high regard, there were no I-told-you-so comments from anyone upon my return in July 2002. However, the RBS experience did leave a scar that took a while to heal. Quite clearly, I wasn't ready for the world outside the police service.

Chapter 19

Eating 'Humble Pie' Is Not Always Bad

Having experienced my ill-fated and self-imposed torture at RBS, I was back with Lancashire Constabulary with immense help and support from Jameel—back where I was welcomed with open arms and valued again, both by my colleagues and senior officers.

This was most apparent with Wendy Walker and the DCC, who later went on to become chief constable of Nottinghamshire. The DCC and I had a healthy respect for each other, although we never really developed the level of close working relationship, I went on to enjoy with DCC Steve Finnigan, who later became chief constable at Lancashire Constabulary. This was mainly due to the different role I moved on to, soon after my return.

The warmth that emanated from Wendy was something I'd never seen from a police officer of her rank; it continued when she became our assistant chief constable (ACC). Her joy and excitement at the successful project I had put together, in partnership with Lancashire Council of Mosques, was sincere and genuine; it provided a real boost to my confidence and lifted my spirits. Wendy willingly shared much of her vast knowledge and willing agreed to chair the working group for the project. She was more a friend than a boss.

Following my 'high-profile' return, with the glad-you're-back welcome and some humble pie eating on my part, I was once more doing the job I loved. I have to say, my smooth return took away all the pain of the previous six months. In my absence, as far as I can recall, Jameel had taken on the mantle admirably. He also openly displayed his delight in my return. Together, we picked up where we had left off.

Building on the foundations I had laid down, before Jameel came to work with me, the two of us were able to attend more events, run more initiatives, build more bridges, encourage more applicants, and recruit more officers than ever before. We were building a significant momentum once again.

Up to that point, our focus had been on attracting and recruiting BAME police officers. Now it was time to get a clear picture of the retention and progression of our BAME officers and to see how we could support their progression. We sat on several of our internal strategic working groups, including the RR&P strategy board, made up of chief officers, representatives of the police authority, community representatives, heads of departments, HR, trade unions, and representatives of the Lancashire Black Police Association (LBPA).

At several of these meetings, data and management reports on the constabulary's workforce were presented. The data showed numbers of BAME, and female officers recruited and promoted, as well as on those who had left. The data showed upwards trends in recruitment but no movement in progression.

In 2002, the highest ranking BAME officer in Lancashire was

an inspector; there were only two throughout the force and just six sergeants. It was pitiful. The progression of BAME officers clearly lacked the same focus, commitment, and energy applied to recruitment.

Along with progression of BAME officers, the other area of major concern was the disproportionate number of BAME officers and staff being referred to the constabulary's Professional Standards Department (PSD). These referrals led to disproportionate investigations, and in turn, disproportionate sanctions imposed on BAME staff. These were some of the issues I would address in my final role with Lancashire Constabulary.

Chapter 20

What, Me a Leader? Who Would Have Believed It!

An unexpected meeting, less than six months after my return to the Constabulary, took place between Jameel; Altaf (Al) Yusuf, a very well-respected colleague; and me, taking my career into another unexpected direction. I thought the meeting was to discuss the planning of a 'multifaith' or 'quiet' room. However, it soon became clear the meeting had been pre-planned by Jameel and Al about the upcoming elections for the executive committee of the Lancashire Black Police Association (LBPA).

All three of us had known for some time there had been a strong feeling among BAME staff that the LBPA was ineffective. It was doing little to bring about a better working environment or address many of the community's issues and concerns. Jameel quickly owned up to the fact that he didn't tell me the real reason for the meeting, as he knew I'd refuse to attend such a meeting. However, after a lengthy discussion, we agreed the only way to bring about change was from within the LBPA.

To do that, we would need people to stand for the executive positions and challenge those currently occupying those positions.

This begged the question, Who?

At that moment, I was certain Jameel was about to tell me he would stand as the chair; after all, he had the charisma, the personality, and the clarity of thought to lead the LBPA.

That's when they both looked at me simultaneously.

'Oh no. Don't look at me. I'm not interested. Besides, I have my hands full with my own role,' I protested.

'You are the ideal person!' Jameel interjected. 'You're highly respected and well known by our staff, the communities, and the chief officer team.'

He went on, 'We all agree how ineffective the LBPA has become. You've said that to me yourself many times. Who else could do it?'

'You!' I replied. 'You have what it takes.'

This fell on deaf ears. 'There are three strategic positions within the LBPA committee that need to be changed—the chair, the general secretary, and the social treasurer,' he said calmly. 'Al will stand for the general secretary's post. I will stand for the social treasurer's post, and we would like you to stand for the chair's post.'

It was obvious my protests were futile, just like all those years ago when I was given no choice but to play in goals. Once again, I felt I was being pushed into something I'd never considered.

Perhaps at this stage it would be helpful if I provide some background to my relationship with the LBPA up to that point.

Although I was a founding member of the LBPA, I had little dealings with it. This went back to the time when it was formed in 1997, when I lacked the confidence to consider any of the roles of a principal officer and played a 'bit part' by becoming a member. Following changes to the executive committee, I slowly drifted away from the LBPA, to the point where I thought the leadership did little to help its cause. I always thought, as a principle, that any support network should seek collective progress and not individual gain, which should be visibly demonstrated by its leadership. It's not what I saw. Rightly or wrongly, I distanced myself from the LBPA.

In my MECLO role, I was so engrossed with my recruitment role that it had never occurred to me to consider any kind of role with the LBPA. Furthermore, I always felt I lacked the skills and confidence required for such roles. Now I was being asked to stand for the position of chair—by two people I trusted highly and whose opinions I valued. I found myself trying to convince them that I lacked leadership qualities. They would hear none of it. Cleverly highlighting my strengths, they pointed out what I had achieved, how good I was with people, and how tactful and diplomatic I was in dealing with the chief officers.

Reluctantly, I agreed to stand.

***

The LBPA was structured in a similar way to the National Black Police Association (NBPA), with the following executive positions:

- Chair
- General Secretary
- Treasurer
- Social Secretary
- Social Treasurer

The elections for the LBPA executive committee took place in April 2003. Both Jameel and I were successful; unfortunately, Al was not.

I was to continue in my role as MECLO and devote four hours per week to the LBPA work.

First meeting with the Chief Constable

Until *that* meeting with Jameel and our colleague, an active role within the LBPA was never a consideration for me. Since my return, I had fully immersed myself in my old job. Yet here I was, the new LBPA chair less than a year into my return. How had this happened? What had I done? I felt both ecstatic and worried sick. I remember saying to myself, *this could be very embarrassing and ruin my reputation, painstakingly built through my work in recruitment.*

I had many doubts about my ability to cope with new role. I shared them with Marge.

She sat me down, looked me in the eye and said, 'You can do it. I have every faith in you. It will be the making of you.'

Those words gave me the inspiration and impetus I needed.

My first job as the newly elected chair of the LBPA was to have a meeting with the then chief constable, Paul Stephenson.

Can you imagine it? I, a mere PC who dreaded going into the sergeant's office, was now about to have a one-to-one with the chief constable of Lancashire Constabulary?

What CC Stephenson said at the start of our meeting momentarily took me by surprise. I was aware of the poor relationship between the LBPA and the constabulary; however, I wasn't prepared for the chief's opening words. The euphoria I'd felt following my 'victory' was instantly deflated, and his words will always live on in my mind.

'Now that you are the LBPA chair, Mebs, what do you want from the constabulary?'

For a few seconds, his words threw me. To my amazement, I remained calm and took my time before replying, 'Sir, to be honest with you, I don't know what I want. There are several things I still need to consider—for example, what the constabulary expects and wants from the LBPA, what the members want, how the LBPA can support your ambition, how the LBPA can help the constabulary improve its service delivery to the BAME communities, and how I can cultivate a professional and productive relationship between us.'

I finished with a huge sigh of relief and wondered, where those words had come from.

CC Stephenson's persona completely changed. It was obvious he wasn't expecting that response. He probably expected another slanging match or unrealistic demands. He relaxed, sat back, and looked me straight in the eye and said, 'Yes of course, and you are going to need time and support in putting something together.'

We then talked more about my vision for the LBPA, the NBPA, and the challenges faced by the police service. I realised then that I had won my first and most important battle. We agreed on a time frame for me to put together a business case for the work I felt was needed and the resources required.

Coming away from that meeting, I felt on top of the world and rather proud of myself. I felt immensely positive about the task and challenges that lay ahead, so different from my outlook in the past.

I couldn't wait to tell the one person who had been instrumental in all of this—Marge.

Mahmood Ahmed

My first LBPA business case

My starting point for the business case was to review what the LBPA currently did and what resources we had. That was quite simple. There was no record of what the LBPA did, so it became a blank canvas for what I wanted to do. As for resources, the LBPA had the following:

- Four hours a week for the chair to conduct LBPA business
- A budget of £3,000 per annum
- A mobile phone
- A laptop

I guess with those resources there was not a lot the previous chair and the executive committee could have done.

However, for me it was not about what you could do given the resources but, rather, what you do to get the required resources. Put another way, it was about the strategy you put in place to get the buy-in from the constabulary to obtain the resources the LBPA needed.

When I put my business case together, I deployed a tactical awareness I didn't know I had. I guess previously there had been no call for it. I ignored the so-called 'confrontational' tactics favoured by many BPAs across the country, which publicly embarrassed their force but yielded little progress. Instead of putting forward what the LBPA wanted, I based the business case on what the constabulary could expect from the LBPA and the resources required for that work, focusing on how the LBPA would support the constabulary with workforce representation and the chief's ambition to be the 'best police force in the country'. The business case I put forward was the most demanding piece of work I had done up to that point; it certainly tested my limited ability, which lacked financial management capability.

Thankfully, I received some very welcome support from Supt Ian Cardwell—someone else to whom I owe a great deal of gratitude. At the time, Ian was head of the Community Safety and Partnerships department, and his first-hand knowledge about the workings of the chief officer team was of significant help with the business case. Ian was a well-liked officer, but his most enduring qualities were his ability to forget about his rank and be approachable, kind, thoughtful, and supportive. That could not be said of many senior police officers, some of whom were totally career-driven and ruthless.

Ian went out of his way to make time for me and to guide me in putting together the business case—such a pity he supported the reds from Merseyside!

I am a very simple, some would say a naive man, but following those opening words, Paul Stephenson was always very fair and honest with me. Like Steve Finnigan, Paul did wonders for my fragile confidence.

In the new business case, I included the following LBPA aims and objectives:

- To be the collective voice for its members
- To help support the constabulary in its ambition to become the best force in the country
- To provide advice, guidance, and support for the LBPA members
- To work with the constabulary to improve its relationship with BAME communities
- To help the constabulary improve service delivery to BAME communities
- To support the constabulary's work on under-representation and the retention and progression of BAME staff

- To help the constabulary create a better working environment for BAME staff
- To build positive relationships with the constabulary, the trade unions, and the other staff support networks
- To raise any issues and concerns professionally, diplomatically, and with sensitivity

To deliver the above piece of work, the following resources were requested:

- A budget of £13,000
- Two and a half days a week for the chair to conduct LBPA business
- Four hours per month for each of the LBPA executive committee members
- The retention of the mobile phone and laptop

When I shared my business case with my fellow executive committee members, they were all shocked. They said the chief officer team and the business group would simply throw it out. I disagreed and said the work we would be undertaking could only benefit the constabulary and would, in the long run, save them money. From now on, we would not be operating as if we were outside the constabulary; we would act as a 'critical friend' to raise our concerns and provide expert advice to the constabulary on issues affecting our BAME staff and our diverse communities.

Without so much as a raised eyebrow, the chief officer team and the business group fully approved the business case, which was met with incredulous disbelief by the LBPA committee.

Following further approval by the constabulary and the LBPA executive committee, I combined my MECLO role with my new role, splitting my working week fifty-fifty between the two roles.

I continued to support Jameel with our engagement and recruitment initiatives. But for my role as the LBPA chair, there were several areas I wanted to look at. I wanted to get a better understanding of some of the challenges my members faced and how our white colleagues viewed the LBPA. I also wanted to promote the work of the LBPA across the constabulary and specialist departments, develop initiatives that would help the progression of BAME staff, represent the LBPA at social events within BAME communities, and organise our own social events so our members could get together and share their experiences and support each other. Finally, I wanted to review the LBPA membership, which at the time excluded our white colleagues.

The work of the LBPA began to grow very quickly. More and more BAME staff joined the LBPA and started to seek our support, which increased our popularity and effectiveness.

The LBPA did not provide legal advice; this was offered by the Police Federation for police officers and by UNISON for police staff. With our knowledge and awareness of the issues faced by our BAME staff, we were better able to support them by acting as a conduit between all parties and started to work hand in hand with the Federation and UNISON.

To avoid any misunderstanding or potential tension between the LBPA and the trade unions, I arranged personal meetings with their principal officers to share my vision for the LBPA and to clarify any ambiguity. Both welcomed this fresh approach and readily offered their support. This was beginning to work so well I was getting regular calls

Mahmood Ahmed

for advice and support from them both, asking me to attend disciplinary meetings and investigations involving BAME staff.

This special relationship went from strength to strength and was the envy of many BPAs and trade unions across the country, as I later found out from some of my NBPA colleagues.

However, some of this work had to be put on hold, within six months of becoming the LBPA chair, I was faced with two events that needed my immediate first, events that perhaps helped define my leadership.

Chapter 21

The Secret Policeman Documentaries

I was beginning to find my feet in my new role, further encouraged by my successful first meeting with our chief constable and the successful outcome of my first ever business case, whilst still delivering on my MECLO role in the recruitment department.

But just as things were going well, two events surfaced to test my resolve. The first was another devastating blow for everyone involved with the police service.

In October 2003, the BBC aired a controversial and provocative documentary, *The Secret Policeman*. It featured investigative reporter Mark Daly, who revealed racism among police recruits at a police training centre. For years BAME staff, the NBPA, and the local BPAs had been raising the issue of racism within the police service, without the level of impact this documentary had, not since the Stephen Lawrence murder.

Daly went undercover to investigate, at first-hand, to what level progress had been made since the Macpherson recommendations. He took the unusual step of applying to become a police officer with Greater Manchester Police—seeing for himself how the whole process of recruitment and training took place. Having successfully completed the recruitment process, he began his initial training at Bruche Training Centre—the same centre I'd attended in 1989. During his training, he secretly filmed the behaviour and language of some of the new recruits.

Daly's film revealed shocking and damning evidence of blatant racism. Although no one could deny it existed previously, it was now on film for millions to see on national TV. The then home secretary, David Blunkett, and various chief officers came out condemning the graphic images of police officers engaged in racist discussions.

To say the programme caused uproar in the media would be an understatement—with sensational headlines in every media outlet. The revelations once again highlighted the fragile relationship between the police and BAME communities. It also, quite naturally, had an unsettling effect on BAME staff. To add to their woes, there were some senior officers who were too quick to come out with defensive statements, such as, 'A few rotten apples doesn't make the whole police service racist.' They were ill-advised. Being defensive at the time did little to inspire confidence. A collective condemnation by rank and file would have helped. Were this followed by public apology by each individual chief constable, along with an expression of determination to root out racism from within each force may have gone some way towards reassuring BAME staff and communities.

I have always failed to understand why so many in the police service find it immensely difficult to say they are sorry when wrong. In my view, there has never been a better example of this than the Hillsborough disaster in 1989, which resulted in deaths of ninety-six football fans.

Grave mistakes were made by senior officers, yet there was the 'closing of ranks' and altering of statements. An unreserved apology should have been the least the families deserved. It was shameful.

For the BAME staff, the documentary had only managed to highlight a tip of the iceberg. Some didn't dare publicly express this, for fear of repercussions. This was left to the NBPA and the local BPAs, who did not hesitate to unite in their condemnation.

When the documentary was aired, I was on leave. I received a call asking me to return to work immediately. I was told to work with our chief officer team to provide support and reassurances for our BAME staff and communities.

Before agreeing to do this, I pointed the danger of 'shallow words' to our chief officer team. With their reassurances, I worked with our media team to develop and put out several internal and external messages. Accompanied by a member of the chief officer team, I met several staff and members of the community face to face to listen to what they had to say and to reassure them.

This was a delicate matter. I needed to find the right balance between how it was within the constabulary and to provide meaningful and genuine assurance messages. Having worked on what I was wanted to say, I managed to find the words I was happy with. I did not simply want to go along with what the constabulary wanted to say, as it was important to demonstrate to our BAME staff and our communities that the LBPA understood how they felt and why and that we were there to ensure the constabulary understood too. After initial reluctance and suspicion, meetings with our BAME staff and communities slowly began to take place, as did their desire to vent their understandable anger.

Following the programme, our workforce initiatives took a hit, as they did across the country. Some BPAs began to ask themselves whether they should continue to support the police service with these initiatives. One or two publicly stopped doing so, until the police service took a more robust approach to dealing with racism. A similar debate took place in Lancashire. However, we concluded that we would continue to support our force, as we didn't believe that withdrawing our support would be in the best interests of our members in the long run. The documentary provided an opportunity to make greater demands from the constabulary on accountability and the way it should deal with racism.

It is true to say that, following the programme, some of our BAME staff were reluctant to report incidents of racism or to approach the LBPA for support, fearing repercussions from their colleagues and the force. Those who did seek support wanted to do so well away from police premises, nervously looking over their shoulders for any prying eyes. Some felt that simply talking to the LBPA would make them a target. This was a huge setback for both the constabulary and the LBPA. It felt like starting all over again, trying to win back their trust and confidence, but it was totally rational.

This emphasised how important it was to keep any support I provided strictly confidential, even from my own executive committee. A few of the members said they would stop all contact with the LBPA if their privacy was compromised. Their trust of the LBPA was at a low ebb; their trust of the police service was at rock bottom. Who could blame them?

Fortunately, none of the officers accused of racism in the programme were from Lancashire, and there were no new recruits from Lancashire within Mark Daly's intake. Slowly, as I persisted with winning back the members' trust, over a period of months, they began to see the LBPA's efforts to help them, to try to improve their working environment, and to provide a better service for our BAME communities were sincere.

***

Along with many other people, I have often condemned the media for their sensational headlines in efforts to sell a story. However, in this case, Mark Daly went to great lengths and took huge personal risks in highlighting the depth of racism within the police service. I applaud Mr Daly's actions.

Chapter 22

The National Black Police Association

The National Black Police Association (NBPA) was formed in the 1990s. It acted as an umbrella organisation, advising, supporting, and liaising with policing ministers, all police forces, and local BPAs across the country. It has provided a collective voice for all the local BPAs and given strength and encouragement to other staff support networks too. All this was done by some who endured great personal hurt and pain, stress, and anxiety.

The NBPA was officially launched in November 1998, fully supported and funded by the Home Office. Although I went to the launch of the NBPA with my son Bashir, it was more for the sake of networking rather than any real interest in its work. At the time, I was an operational officer and, following my experiences with my local BPA, showed, rather naively, little interest in the workings or needs for such a national body.

During the event, I heard several horror stories of blatant racism, but still the timing was not yet right for me to get involved. As they say, 'Things happen to you when you are ready.' I wasn't ready. I was still not aware of the bigger picture, which can happen if you work in isolation. This, due to our small numbers, happened to a lot of BAME officers. If you didn't come across racism yourself or didn't hear about it, then you thought perhaps it didn't exist.

My thoughts on racism began to change when I moved to our HQ in 1999. Within this new role, I started not only to deal with other BAME staff, but also to also hear about some of the issues they were facing. My dealings with the BAME public and visits to other forces opened my eyes further to some of the challenges BAME officers and staff faced on a regular basis. These included 'monkey noises', other name-calling, exclusion from team events, marginalisation, constant degrading comments, bacon sandwiches left in Muslim and Sikh officers' lockers, regularly being overlooked for promotion or secondments to specialist posts.

Furthermore, as chair of the LBPA, I was the Lancashire representative on the NBPA's national executive committee (NEC), enabling me to attend their NEC quarterly meetings, which provided a safe platform for attendees to share their horrific stories.

The NBPA has had a difficult history. But since I became chair of the LBPA, it has had my support.

However, some of those involved with the NBPA movement came with their own history of issues and difficult times as police officers and staff, some facing racial discrimination on a regular basis. For a few, this had happened throughout their careers. If they raised racism as an issue, they were met with a brick wall; those around them closed ranks, and they were often labelled as troublemakers. Their resilience was tested to the limit. It is understandable that a few saw an opportunity or succumbed to 'lashing out' or 'saying it as it was'. They were seen as airing their dirty linen publicly. It is too easy to label them as 'unprofessional'. Unfortunately, in my view, it only served to alienate them and the NBPA even further.

Although I understood and sympathised with what they had gone through, I didn't believe such tactics would bring about the required change within the police service. I've had numerous debates and discussions with some of my NBPA colleagues on this issue; it is fair to say not all agreed with me—especially in my early days when I lacked the confidence to articulate a more convincing argument.

However, this brings me to the second major event that took place within my first two years as the LBPA chair.

The NBPA comes to Lancashire

Within eighteen months of taking over as the LBPA chair, both Mr Finnigan and the Lancashire Police Authority (LPA) agreed to host the NBPA AGM and conference, against my advice. I was against it not because Lancashire Constabulary wasn't ready, but because I wasn't ready. Thankfully, both Mr Finnigan and the LPA felt a national event would be good for Lancashire Constabulary and raise our profile and highlight the good work we were doing.

However, hosting the event required a huge amount of work for the NBPA and the LBPA It meant organising, coordinating, and liaising with forces and other partners; identifying and inviting keynote speakers and dignitaries; pulling together sponsorship packages; seeking auction and raffle prizes; and managing the logistics of pulling the whole event together. I have to say, both the NBPA and our own general secretary worked tirelessly to make the event a success.

Mahmood Ahmed

I had successfully argued for our general secretary to be seconded to the AGM and conference planning and implementation group on a full-time basis. He had exceptional event planning and networking skills, which proved to be great assets for us all. One of my failings at the time was not to recognise and fully show my appreciation of those skills to him. It was another lesson learned on reflection.

The NBPA AGM and conference was held in October 2004, at the Imperial Hotel, Blackpool. As host and LBPA chair, I was required to welcome everyone to the event and deliver the opening speech. The thought simply terrified me, leading to many sleepless nights. *What have I got myself into?* I asked myself. In attendance were representatives from the Home Office, local politicians, Mr Finnigan, the High Sheriff of Lancashire, Police Authority representatives, chief officers from other forces, prominent members of the community, NBPA officials, representatives of BPAs across the country, our own BPA officials and members, and other invited guests. There were almost five hundred people in attendance—including the media. Never one for the limelight, I was a nervous wreck, right up to the moment I got up to make my welcoming speech.

As I was introduced to the stage, something truly remarkable happened to me, something difficult to explain, just like that time when I saw Shantilal in a different light at school all those years ago. I got up from my seat, and as I was making my way towards the stage, I took a deep breath and realised I had to do this. I had to deliver a composed and measured speech. I knew that, not only did my reputation depend on it, but so did that of the LBPA and, more importantly, that of my force. I had spent weeks writing and practising the biggest speech of my life.

After managing to maintain my composure and get through perhaps the longest fifteen minutes of my policing career, I took a deep breath and stepped away from the podium and hoped my words made sense. I then went into unconscious shutdown; I remember nothing of the other speeches—even though, to my sheer delight and huge relief, there were people on their feet, giving me a standing ovation. My heart was beating so rapidly I thought it was going to explode. Later, many in the audience came up to me with complimentary and kind words that have remained with me, none more so than the following:

- 'The Lancashire BPA has gone right up there in my estimation.' (Senior NBPA committee member)
- 'That was a very statesmanlike speech.' (Police Authority member)
- 'For the first time, as a white officer I was made to feel proud to be at the NBPA event.' (Several senior and rank-and-file white officers)

For others, something like this may represent a modest achievement, but for someone like me, it was more than I'd dared to hope for.

The NBPA conference was deemed a success, and I owe my gratitude to our general secretary, the NBPA team, Mr Finnigan, the Lancashire Police Authority, and all who worked tirelessly to make it happen.

To my knowledge, it is a privilege Lancashire has managed only once.

Following the conference, I began to pay more attention to the NBPA movement and to feel more comfortable in attending their NEC meetings. These meetings were held, initially, at the most central point of the country to make it easier for all to attend and, later, within those forces whose BPA agreed to meet the cost of hosting such meetings.

As the years went by, I went from a bit player to someone who was beginning to have more and more influence on the NBPA. Gradually, I was being invited by principal officers to spend more time with them in London to support them. Their confidence and trust in me had grown rapidly, to such an extent that they even asked me to help deal with some of the executive team's internal issues.

Unfortunately, sometime later, the Home Office withdrew its funding for the NBPA, amid allegations of mismanagement of funds. It must be pointed out that an inquiry into such allegations completely exonerated the NBPA. Nevertheless, the Home Office upheld its decision, and the NBPA now had to raise its own funds. It did this by charging local BPAs annual subscription fees, generating funds from its AGMs, and delivering training packages.

I helped to set up the first NBPA scrutiny committee and was elected its vice chair and, later, chair. I was becoming not only trusted but also respected by those at the top of the organisation. Gradually, more and more people were now asking me to stand as the NBPA president or at least consider one of the other executive committee positions. I have to say I was very tempted. However, during my meetings with Mr Finnigan, I had given him my word that I would stay at Lancashire and complete the work I had started. I would not break my word.

Some of my friends and colleagues advised me to think through my decision carefully, pointing out how much more I could do at the national level. When I turned down opportunity after opportunity, some questioned my lack of ambition or desire to take up such a high-profile role. But I was not driven by such personal ambition; I valued loyalty above my ambition. My father's words were always there as a reminder: 'Your word is your bond. Never break it.'

I have tried to remain true to what my father said to me. I had given my word to Steve Finnigan, and I remained with Lancashire Constabulary and the LBPA until my retirement in 2013.

***

'Come on over, Mebs. It would be lovely to see you.'

As mentioned above, I would occasionally spend time in the NBPA offices in London to support their work. While working there one day, I was asked by the NBPA coordinator to help set up a meeting with the new deputy commissioner of the Metropolitan Police—my former chief, Paul Stephenson. Apparently, a meeting between them had been proving elusive, and they felt they were being given the run around. I rang Mr Stephenson from the NBPA office on his personal mobile number, which he had kindly given me. He answered immediately. I said I was in London and asked if there was any chance of seeing him. Despite the short notice, he agreed straight away, saying, 'Come on over, Mebs. It would be lovely to see you.'

My NBPA colleagues were amazed. My ability to see the Met's deputy commissioner at such short notice gave me further credence in their eyes.

Of course, Mr Stephenson only agreed to see me so readily because of our previous relationship and because of the man he was. Our relationship, based on mutual trust and respect, had blossomed, so much so that, before he left Lancashire, he had asked me to be his informal advisor on matters of race and the BPA.

Mahmood Ahmed

I had learned the importance of building meaningful relationships, from my early days on the Grange and Franklands beat in Preston.

My former chief was delighted to see me and made me very welcome in his impressive office at the New Scotland Yard. We talked a while about Lancashire Constabulary and his new role, before discussing the business at hand. I asked him outright if I could help facilitate meetings between him and the NBPA. He said he was reluctant to meet with the NBPA until he had a better understanding of what the organisation wanted from a meeting with him. He also asked if I could provide a clear agenda from the NBPA and be present during the meetings, at least initially. I agreed to do both.

New acting chief constable for Lancashire Constabulary

When Paul Stephenson took up his new position as the deputy commissioner at the Met in 2005, Lancashire Constabulary appointed Steve Finnigan as the acting chief constable and, in March 2007, as our chief constable.

It was under Steve Finnigan's leadership that my confidence really began to grow in dealing with the chief officer team. Steve allowed a close relationship to develop between us. He was the one who opened many strategic doors for me, inviting me to sit on many of the constabulary's forums. He had already set up regular meetings between us whilst he was deputy chief constable; they continued when he became our chief constable.

He always made me feel valued, making time to listen to what I had to say. At times what I said to him must have been at odds with what he heard from his senior officers and his chief officer team. Yet, he knew I had no axes to grind, though I can't say Steve was regularly hearing from his yes-men, —I said it as I saw it, perhaps still showing my innocence.

Through my interactions with other BPAs across the country, I realised how incredibly fortunate I was to have had a two uncommonly supportive chief constables to work with.

I have been to several NBPA conferences and AGMs, but I have never seen other chief constables behave as Steve Finnigan did at one of their conferences in Manchester. I wish I could remember the year.

However, during the lunch break Steve asked me if some of my colleagues from the NBPA would like to join him for lunch, away from the venue. He said he wanted to hear different perspectives about the NBPA and the local BPAs. He treated a group of about eight of us to lunch and listened intently to what people had to say. All my colleagues were impressed with his sincerity and desire to engage with them.

On a personal level, Steve was incredibly supportive when my son Bashir was diagnosed with cancer, contacting me personally to tell me to take as long as required to look after him and not worry about rushing back to work.

Steve and I also shared a love of football, despite him being a blue from Merseyside. He had played at a much higher level than me, playing for the England police team. Steve once told me, 'Mebs, play as long as you can.' I did, right up to my mid-fifties.

Inputs on behalf of the NBPA to newly qualified superintendents

Off the back of my increasing role for the NBPA, I was asked to deliver inputs to the newly qualified superintendents and their police staff equivalents at the national police training centre (now the College of

Policing) in Ryton near Coventry. The aim of this was to help raise funds; these inputs generated £400 plus accommodation, per session for the NBPA, with three inputs each year.

The College of Policing asked the NBPA to deliver these inputs as part of the diversity training on its Tomorrow's Leadership programme. I was given no brief by the NBPA, apart from a few words from then general secretary, Stafford Brooks, who simply told me, 'Mebs, just do the same stuff you do in Lancashire; they'll find it refreshing.'

Stafford Brooks, what a fine gentleman. I feel few words about my dear friend Stafford are appropriate.

Stafford was a detective from Staffordshire—seriously, he worked for Staffordshire Police! He was the chair of their Multi-Cultural Association (Staffordshire's equivalent to a local BPA). Stafford was huge man in every sense. He was huge in stature, with a personality to match, and hugely popular with everyone. He was also an immensely talented musician. I was and still am in awe of Stafford. Like many people from an African Caribbean background, he had a great deal of natural charisma and zest for life. For all the compliments he paid me and the mutual respect we had for each other, I'd love to have had an ounce of his charisma.

Back to the inputs, there were twenty-four individuals on each course, split into groups of four. Each group was given an hour's input by the 'experts' representing either a staff support network, their community, or a relevant external support organisation.

As I had no brief, I based my inputs on the work I had started to do in Lancashire, having authentic and honest conversations with officers from sergeants to chief inspector levels. These inputs were not to be confused with inputs to new recruits. These inputs or sessions were more a 'facilitation and exploration' of some difficult aspects of diversity, including the need for staff support networks; BAME race, religion, and culture; representative workforce challenges; racism; the MacPherson report; political correctness; and the 'old boy's network' within the police service.

The ground rules were drawn up by the participants, but I insisted they formed the basis of a safe learning environment. We also followed the Chatham House Rules, allowing people to feel comfortable in sharing their thoughts and respecting their confidentiality.

From my own experiences of diversity training within the police service, I wanted to get away from ramming legislation down people's throats. I knew people were genuinely concerned about getting things wrong and fearful of making mistakes when talking about difference. Creating a safe learning environment enabled the participants to ask difficult questions and explore their thoughts without being judged or labelled.

Despite the ground rules and the safe learning environment, it was still difficult initially to get them to speak freely. To help, I would start by sharing my thoughts on many areas of policing, my ignorance, my fears, and my areas of vulnerability.

I was not surprised to learn that many of them hadn't had any meaningful conversations or discussions with their own staff support networks, due to their own uncomfortableness at engaging with them. Some said their negative perceptions of the support networks put them off. A few felt they didn't see the BPAs advancing the cause for BAME staff, the police, or the BAME communities. A few said they kept away from their BPAs altogether.

When I shared some of the work that the LBPA was doing, most said they would encourage their BPAs to do the same. At the end of the sessions, they were very complementary. Many felt that, for the first time, they were able to have an in-depth discussion on areas in which they previously felt ill at ease.

For me, it was all about winning hearts and minds, providing a different perspective to the ones they'd arrived with, and leaving them with decisions to make about if and how they would engage with their BPAs and other staff support networks.

Several of the attendees kept in touch, offering to mentor some of the Lancashire BAME officers seeking promotion or lateral progression. A few of our officers took up these opportunities, but many more were concerned about seeking support from outside the force, fearing it might go against them.

Unfortunately, this piece of work came much too close to my retirement to have made any significant impact on the wider policing service—it was a drop in the ocean compared with what was needed really.

Chapter 23

Consolidation and Next Steps for the LBPA

Having survived *The Secret Policeman* and successfully hosted the NBPA AGM and conference in 2003 and 2004 respectively, my thoughts turned to what was next for the LBPA.

By 2005, I had held the LBPA chair's position for two years, without challenge from anyone. However, the workload from my two roles was becoming unmanageable; therefore, it was time to decide which one I wanted to commit to.

To make the decision, I arranged two meetings—one with the LBPA executive committee and the other with our chief constable, Paul Stephenson.

The LBPA committee gave me its full backing, acknowledging the slowly changing perceptions of the LBPA, but agreed there was still a lot of work ahead of us.

CC Stephenson thanked me for my work in both roles, but he was also more direct and asked me what I wanted to do. Unlike my first meeting with him, this time, I was well prepared, decisive, and clear. I wanted the challenge presented by the LBPA and told Mr Stephenson that, if I were to continue as chair, the current resources needed to be reviewed.

He simply replied, 'Then you know what you have to do.'

I did.

In 2005, with the executive committee's backing and support from Supt Ian Cardwell, I put forward a second business case. Once again, it was fully approved, resulting in the following resources:

- One full-time officer
- A fully equipped office for two members of staff
- A budget of £13,000

Having secured the business case, I now needed to draw up a new vision for the LBPA. This would include a marketing strategy and better engagement with our members, operational divisions, specialist departments, and our BAME communities.

My vision for the LBPA was always to broaden our horizons and approach things differently. We would listen to different perspectives, expect positive outcomes, and help others see the LBPA in a different light. Some of my team disagreed with my vision; they argued the LBPA may become a 'nodding dog' or lack 'teeth'. They also felt we should occasionally remind the constabulary why we exist—a reference to how the LBPA had operated in the past.

As mild-mannered as I was and as willing as I was to listen to different perspectives, I was also determined to change the way the LBPA conducted its business, the way it supported its members, and the way it sought to help facilitate differences throughout the constabulary. This meant changing the outlook of both our executive committee and our members. I argued that the way we'd dealt with *The Secret Policeman* and the positive response we received nationally following the NBPA AGM had afforded us a lot of goodwill. Furthermore, the way we were conducting ourselves was a major factor in our business cases being approved.

I told them that, when I took over, it was abundantly clear to me that the force saw the LBPA as a threat rather than an asset, which meant it was viewed with suspicion. I wanted to change that. I wanted the LBPA to be a true critical friend of the constabulary. I suggested that we should save showing 'our teeth' or our resolve as a last resort. I was determined to find a way I was comfortable with; after all, as chair, it would be on my head if things went wrong. Until that point, this kind of thinking had remained absent from the conscious of many within the LBPA.

However, before I could begin my work, we had overlooked one small matter. We all assumed I'd automatically take up the full-time role without going through a selection process. Luckily, it was quickly picked up by an eagle-eyed member of the executive committee, and a proper selection process was put in place.

This process was open to all LBPA executive committee members. Those interested needed to submit an expression of interest. If there was more than one expression of interest, a panel would interview all prospective candidates. As it turned out, there were only two committee members interested in the full-time role—our general secretary and me.

The panel was made up of three people—an LBPA committee member, a HR representative, and the chair of the Black and Asian Police Association (BAPA) from Greater Manchester Police (GMP) (who later went on to become the NBPA president).

Following a successful interview, I took up the full-time post in 2005.

***

Mahmood Ahmed

Having secured a business case and a full-time post for myself, I began work on my vision and a proper plan for the LBPA. Over the period of my tenure, I carried out reviews and developed and put in place the following:

1. *Review of the executive committee tenure.* I felt that twelve months did not give the team enough time. It was, therefore, changed to two years, bringing it in line with the tenure of the NBPA.

2. *Review of the executive committee make-up and introduction of divisional reps.* I wanted to create two new posts on the executive committee and a new post within each operational division:

   - LBPA vice chair—to support my work and provide cover in my absence

   - Training and marketing officer—to deliver inputs to all new recruits and to take on the role of marketing the LBPA internally

   - LBPA divisional reps—to liaise with and provide support to members within their own division and to share local issues and concerns with the LBPA executive committee

3. *Review of membership and introduction of the associate membership.* This was one of the most effective initiatives I implemented. It allowed our white colleagues to join the LBPA as associate members. Many wanted to help and support the work of the LBPA, but as non-members, they were unable to contribute. It also gave them an opportunity to learn about our work and remove some of their negative perceptions about the LBPA.

4. *Introduction of strategic meetings.* For the first time in our history, the LBPA began to hold regular meetings with the chief officer

team, divisional commanders, departmental heads, and other key stakeholders within the force.

Lack of understanding within our specialist departments had been raised with me on several occasions by some of our members, especially within our Professional Standards Department (PSD). A monthly meeting was set up with the department's head, where processes of investigations were outlined and explained to the LBPA, with any disparity and disproportionality raised and discussed. In return, the LBPA delivered presentations to PSD staff on BAME culture and faith, raising their awareness and putting forward secondment opportunities.

Unfortunately, not all heads of departments felt such meetings were necessary; some engaged on an ad hoc basis. I became aware it was going to be a long-term effort. Over time, more and more department heads agreed to hold regular meetings with the LBPA.

5. *Development and implementation of mentoring and secondment opportunities.* Working with the head of learning and development, we developed a training package for BAME staff who wanted to become mentors. Following training they would have the opportunity to mentor new BAME officers and staff. Secondment opportunities with PSD and Special Branch were put in place.

6. *Introduction of additional LBPA executive and divisional rep meetings.* There were no meetings for the LBPA executive committee, only quarterly members' meetings. I felt there was not enough dialogue or flow of information between committee

members. I, therefore, organised monthly meetings between the executive committee and the new divisional reps, followed by quarterly meetings with our members. Regular meetings between the LBPA principal officers allowed me to provide updates on how I was moving the LBPA forward strategically and to receive updates, especially from the divisional reps, who shared any local issues and concerns.

It was here that I met my first challenge. Our members' supervisors didn't want to play ball. They made it difficult for our members to attend meetings, refusing to allow them to attend in duty time or to change their shifts. I had to admit my 'hearts-and-minds' approach failed with some of them. But I had anticipated this, and this was another reason meetings with divisional commanders were set up. If I could get them to see the importance of the LBPA meetings, they could 'encourage' supervisors to allow as many staff as possible to attend. It worked a treat—divisional commanders told all supervisors to plan ahead for these meetings, ensuring adequate cover.

There were workshops within some of our meetings to help support some of our divisional reps to deal with potential backlash from their colleagues or supervisors. Sit saddens me to say that these workshops were needed.

7. *Introduction of new members' meeting venues.* Instead of holding all meetings taking place at our headquarters, they were moved to different divisions, affording opportunities for those who found it difficult to travel to HQ. I also invited divisional commanders to open the meeting with a few words, further providing support and encouragement for our members.

8. *Introduction of attachments and secondments to the LBPA.*
These were offered to BAME staff in unique circumstances—
those under investigations, those awaiting an outcome of an
investigation, those facing a disciplinary hearing, or those
simply off sick. Such a secondment required the approval of their
divisional commander, the HR manager, and the individual
concerned. The length of the secondment was determined by
each individual case, ranging from two days to a week for most
people. However, due to some protracted cases, a few spent the
duration of their investigation on secondment—in some cases,
up to two years—working with me.

How did this benefit the individual or the organisation?

I was aware of the detrimental impact on the individual,
suspended or off sick and awaiting an outcome of an investigation.
I knew that sitting at home, twiddling one's thumbs, and not
knowing what was happening would affect the individual's
morale and well-being, with increased anxiety and stress levels.

An opportunity to contribute whilst the investigation was
ongoing, away from their usual place of work, helped take
people's mind off things. Skilful conversations also allowed
them to discuss issues that concerned them at their own pace,
earning their trust, providing confidentiality, and rebuilding
their confidence. This all contributed greatly to helping them
return to work in a better frame of mind.

All who were given this opportunity were incredibly positive
about their secondment. For many, it cut short their sickness
period by weeks and months. It also saved the constabulary
money in the long run.

9. *Introduction of development and attachment opportunities for white staff to the LBPA.* The previous initiative supported BAME staff. This initiative was aimed at our white colleagues who were given sanctions for low-level inappropriate behaviour and/or comments. I had witnessed many investigations where individuals had been found guilty. They were given 'words of advice', entry was made on their personnel file, and they were told not to do it again. This response did little for their learning and failed to change their behaviour.

I wanted to do something about that. I wanted to help them reflect on what they had done, learn about the impact on their victims, and change their behaviour. Again, with support from divisional commanders, HR managers, and the individuals concerned, a short secondment to the LBPA was offered.

While on secondment, they were given a short development plan that included the following elements:

- Clarification and understanding of why they were there
- A discussion on BAME race, religion or belief, and culture
- Input on support networks and their role within the police service
- The opportunity to explore the Impact of inappropriate language or behaviour
- The opportunity to discuss/debate historical and current issues affecting the police service
- Discussion on issues raised by the individual
- An opportunity to share their personal journey and challenges within the police service
- Feedback from individuals

For the plan to be effective, it had to be conducted in a safe learning environment, in which the individual's understanding was further explored through discussions without being judged. The plan could be extended, shortened, or postponed, depending on the individual or operational needs.

Following the completion of the secondment, due to confidentiality, only generic feedback was provided to divisional HR and the individual's supervision.

All those who took up this initiative willingly became LBPA associate members and said they had a much clearer understanding of the impact of their actions on the victims. Before their secondment, they were all against any kind of staff networks in the police service. This view changed at the end of their secondment; all understood the need for such staff support networks.

10. *Development and implementation of input and presentations to middle management.* I was constantly told by my members that they faced a lot of opposition and negativity from middle management—sergeants and inspectors. I, therefore, organised workshops aimed at these two ranks. These workshops would help raise their understanding of the LBPA and their BAME staff and allowed the LBPA to engage with them on areas they previous felt uncomfortable in.

Below are some of the comments on the feedback from those who attended these workshops:

- 'I never thought I would be able to ask the questions I did today for fear of being labelled.'
- 'This was diversity training as it should be.'

- • 'I now have a much better understanding of my BAME colleagues.'

'There should be more workshops like this, encouraging people to have more open and honest conversations.'

I also started to deliver presentations on the role of the LBPA to new recruits, initially on my own but later with the LBPA's training and marketing officer. The incumbent of this new role was a very articulate woman, helping to further professionalise the LBPA and its workings.

11. *Review and building of meaningful relationships with the unions.* I was aware of the LBPA's fractured relationship with the constabulary. However, I was not aware of the nearly non-existent relationship with the two main trade unions. In fact, one of them told me the relationship was so bad they were considering taking legal action against the LBPA. Thankfully, following my lengthy discussions, this threat was averted.

It was also clear to me that both the Police Federation and UNISON felt threatened by the emergence of a support network like the LBPA. Both were very guarded in our initial meetings. Following detailed and clear outlining on the LBPA's role and our boundaries, I was able to convince them that working together would only benefit our collective members. We would provide the knowledge and expertise on the unique challenges faced by BAME staff, and they would provide the legal expertise. This led to us all working together, with the LBPA attending many disciplinary hearings and meetings, collectively representing our members.

12. *Review and strengthening of relationships with our BAME communities.* Until my appointment, the LBPA had no external focus and little contact with our BAME communities. I wanted to change that. I enrolled the LBPA as a member of several external BAME organisations. This led to invitations to sit on their boards and to attend many of their events, where I was often asked to deliver speeches or presentations, cementing our relationship.

As a final note, in fairness to the previous chairs and the executive committees, they had neither the resources nor the time to be able to consider many of the initiatives I was able to develop and implement.

***

I had realised early on that I could never control the behaviour of some of the racists. But I could perhaps change the mindsets of a few of those I interacted with and begin to have open and honest conversations. What was important to me was to work with those BAME officers and staff who came to seek my help and advice; to help create or increase their resilience; to help them to deal with accepting the dangers of the 'victim mentality'; and to help them build their confidence and self-esteem again. I wanted to help them to understand the following saying: 'It's not what others say or do that is important, but your response to it.'

I wanted to help them to respond to acts of racism appropriately— to show them that they were much stronger than the racists; to help them learn to articulate their arguments; to build their confidence and skills so they could hold difficult conversations on race, and skin colour, and difference—so that they could raise their head above the parapet without it being shot off. Furthermore, I wanted to provide an opportunity for those good people—and there were an awful lot more of those than the racists—to learn about what they were going through, and I wanted to support them. For me, it was the silent majority that held the key when it came to addressing and confronting all aspects of discrimination. I tried to teach them to understand the racist's behaviour; if they could understand it, they could deal it with much more effectively.

My approach slowly began to work, both with the BAME officers and staff who came for support and with the white officers and staff who had the courage to engage with me to learn about difference.

Did it eradicate racism? I hear you ask. Unfortunately, much, much better people than me have been unable to eradicate racism. I was only able to provide a small measure of comfort for those who came to the LBPA—in an effort to help them become more resilient and stronger within themselves. Furthermore, I was able to bring about a change in the thinking and attitude of a small number of our non-BAME officers and staff.

Chapter 24

Counterterrorism

On 11 September 2001—or '9/11' as it became be known—two commercial planes were deliberately crashed into the World Trade Center's Twin Towers in New York, changing the world's perspective and response to terrorism forever. The then American president, George Walker Bush, described the United States' response as a 'war on terror'.

Al-Qaeda, a broad-based militant Islamist organisation was founded by Osama bin Laden in the late 1980s. It began as a logistical network to support Muslims fighting against the Soviet Union's invasion of Afghanistan and transformed it into an active terrorist organisation, carrying out several attacks—including 9/11.

Those and the anthrax attacks, in the same year, increased the fear of nonconventional weapons. It reached a crescendo with the 2002 Iraqi Disarmament Crisis and the 'alleged' weapons of mass destruction being stockpiled. This became the primary justification for the invasion of Iraq in 2003 by American and British forces—an invasion that proved to be illegal, as no such weapons were ever found.

Mahmood Ahmed

If the British government of the time, led by Tony Blair, had any reservations about how to respond to terrorism, several suicide bombings at different locations in London on 7 July 2005, the '7/7 bombings', left it in no doubt.

The government hastily passed several pieces of legislation, which increased powers for the intelligence and secret services. In many people's views, the government then followed whichever direction America took in dealing with terrorism, without the resolve to challenge it.

***

Since 9/11, the 7/7 bombings, and the Iraq War, many countries in the west faced growing numbers of young people becoming radicalised. It is with this in mind that I put forward my thoughts on the causes of how some young Muslims have become radicalised and how we can prevent others from following the same path

My focus here is purely on young Muslims, although some aspects can and do apply to all who have been radicalised.

These thoughts are based on my experiences working with many young Muslims and listening to their views and thoughts through workshops and debates over several years. They are also based on what I've observed in many densely populated areas of Lancashire and Bradford and are snapshots of what many young Muslims have experienced. I believe them to be true reflections of what many go through as they seek to make sense of the impact of many complicated factors they're required to navigate while growing up in multicultural Britain.

The Radicalisation Process

As the 'war on terror' continues, some Arab countries have experienced civil unrest leading to formations of different factions, some based on religious lines. Countries like Syria have seen the rise of Islamic fundamentalists such as the Islamic State of Iraq and Syria (ISIS). This is a group that has attracted young Muslims from many different countries, including Britain.

Why would young Muslims, born and bred in this country, fall prey to being radicalised and attracted to this extremist group? How could the minds of these youngsters be exploited to such an extent where they would be willing to kill many innocent people and take their own lives?

Keeping my focus on the young Muslims in this country and to help find some answers, I explore some of the changes young Muslims have gone through, following their family's migration to this country.

In 1945, following the Second World War, Britain had been left with an overwhelming labour shortage. This shortage was filled significantly by migrants, particularly from the Asian subcontinent, Africa, and the Caribbean.

These migrants did their best to settle into their new lives while maintaining many aspects of their culture and faith. The first generation were mostly men who saw their 'stay' in this country as temporary. Most of them dealt with inequality and discrimination by turning the other cheek. They were law-abiding and kept to themselves, hardly ever coming to the attention of the authorities.

As time went by and many saw chances of returning to their homelands diminishing, thoughts of family and permanency came to the fore. Many had their families join them.

Education allowed many to integrate well with the British way of life and adjust to the challenges posed by the coming together of different cultures. However, the second, third, and even fourth generations born and educated in this country saw issues of inequality and discrimination differently to their parents and grandparents. Most were able to cope with these and the different cultures by living parallel lives—behaving like their parents at home and like other schoolchildren, friends, and colleagues when at school, work, or out socialising.

Most, but not all.

For some their strict upbringing, the confinements of their religion, and pressures from parents, extended family, and the community to conform became too much. For some time, many went along with what was laid out and expected of them. They accepted studying subjects chosen for them, they accepted careers chosen for them, and they accepted arranged marriages—in some cases, forced marriages. The vast majority accepted their fate and the turmoil taking place within in silence. A small number ended up with mental health issues; some turned to drugs and alcohol to cope. A few ended up in petty crime or seeking attention in other ways.

Disillusioned with what their family, their community and their life offered them or disenchanted with the way they were being discriminated against, marginalised, and isolated, a small number began to search for another way out. They had no sense of belonging, no purpose, and no identity. With anger and resentment in their hearts, they felt abandoned. Desperately seeking ways to redeem themselves, they were already angry and bitter towards the authorities, the society, and even their own families and community. This small group, in my view, were the ones who became the most vulnerable to radicalisation and exploitation. They wanted to belong, to feel worthy, and to earn some respect and self-esteem. The only way they felt they could ever achieve this was through sacrificing themselves. Perhaps then they could be seen as having done something worthwhile.

I believe they may have gone through all or some of the scenarios outlined below before being radicalised. These scenarios are based on the accounts of young people whose friends and/or siblings were radicalised or who came to the attention of the intelligence services. I must emphasise that these findings are based on tiny numbers:

1. I am a teenager. I overhear my parents discussing my marriage; due to my cultural norms, I do not have a say in it. Going against my parents is not an option, as it would bring shame to my family. It plays on my mind. Some of my friends advise me to run away, but it is something I cannot bring myself to do. Mainstream services don't understand what I'm going through needs. Where do I go for help?

2. I am a young teenager / young person. Because of my skin colour, religion, and name, my white friends and colleagues are always putting me down. Furthermore, I get no response from the hundreds of job applications I've made. On several occasions, I've been attacked by white youths, simply for being me. The police pay little attention to my complaints; my parents tell me to keep my head down; and my friends tell me to stand up for myself, join a gang, and hit back—none of which helps me. Who do I turn to?

3. I am a student. I have gone against my parents' wishes and dress in Western clothes. I do as much as I can to fit in; I even drink alcohol. Yet on several occasions, I find myself excluded

from certain events and gatherings. I hear my white friends making condescending and hurtful remarks about people from my background. When I confront them, I am told I am overreacting. Sometimes they say, 'But you're not like that. You're all right.' I see inflammatory media headlines about my community being 'welfare cheats'. We are blamed for taking white people's jobs and homes, for being a drain on the NHS, and for any increase in crime. I find it difficult to talk to my parents. Some of my friends say, 'What did you expect? You did turn your back on your own kind.' I feel hopeless and that I've lost my way. Where do I go from here?

4. I have studied hard and gained a degree, yet I am unable to find a job. I've not worked since graduation, even though I've submitted applications for jobs without qualifications. Yet rarely do I get an interview. Many people tell me, 'They see your name and remove you from the recruitment process.' You hear this over and over, and you begin to believe it. Everything seems to be a struggle just because of who I am. It all seems hopeless. Who is going to give me a job? I'm totally demoralised.

It's easy to understand how, when faced with some or all of the above circumstances, young people become vulnerable to those seeking to exploit them. What can be done to support these young people and others falling into the same trap?

There isn't one silver bullet for these complex issues. Having listened to dozens of young people and some of their families, I believe a holistic approach is required. I would suggest several initiatives/programmes outlined below.

Education

I propose a comprehensive suite of educational programmes, which would help to bridge the gap of understanding between different cultures. Most existing programmes are aimed primarily at the young, who are vulnerable to exploitation. But in my view, the needs of both the young people and their parents need to be considered.

The programme aims to:

- Enable both youngsters and their parents to understand Britain's modern society and the challenges posed by different cultures, helping youngsters understand what their parents have gone through, the sacrifices they have made, and what their culture and faith means to them and helping parents understand what it's like for their children to grow up and live in an environment of different cultures and the pressures this duality creates
- Enable both to understand the impact of arranged marriages (where families introduce potential spouses and children choose) and forced marriages (where children are forced to marry someone of their parents' choice) and the complicated correlation between these and the family honour that follows when children go against their parents' wishes
- Enable parents to understand the limiting impact of making career choices for their children
- Enable both to understand the importance of talking and listening to each other, encouraging both parents and their children to share stories and tales from the past and the present and to share some of the challenges they both faced

Mahmood Ahmed

Mentoring

This initiative would allow young people to learn from those who may have experienced some or several of these issues themselves, allowing the young people to find a safe space to share and explore their needs and concerns, whilst being helped to build their confidence and self-esteem.

The programme aims to:

- Provide help and support
- Build confidence and self-esteem
- Provide a safe environment for them to share their experiences, concerns, and issues
- Help them grow and develop

Heritage/identity

History plays an important role in teaching us about where we've come from and the journeys made by those around us and helping us better understand where we're trying to get to. Many Muslim youngsters are not afforded the opportunity to learn these lessons.

The programme aims to:

- Enable youngsters to learn about what it was like for their parents and grandparents when they first came to this country and about the life they left behind
- Provide speakers to share their experiences
- Run workshops on the subcontinent cultures, traditions, and faiths
- Encourage dialogue, perspectives, and debate on heritage and identity

Equality, diversity, and inclusion

From my experience of many Asian parents and some young people, their understanding of diversity usually only encompasses race and religion. This programme would broaden their understanding of equality, diversity, and inclusion, incorporating all protected characteristics within the Equality Act 2010.

This programme will be for both parents and children, with aims to:

- Enable parents to have a basic understanding what these terms mean and how they relate to them and enable children to have a more in-depth understanding of these terms, including prejudice, bias, and discrimination, and how to deal with discrimination
- Enable both to understand that diversity is much broader than just their race and faith

Employment

This programme is aimed at youngsters but would be available to everyone who is unemployed; it involves more than just providing employment skills, as many Muslim youngsters receive extraordinarily little support and advice from their parents.

The programme aims to:

- Increase understanding of how having a job or working can have a positive impact on our lives, our health, and our well-being—providing us the freedom to make lifestyle choices

Mahmood Ahmed

- Provide help and support with jobs searches, filling in applications, and preparing for interviews and assessments
- Encourage feedback and deal with unsuccessful applications

Integration and community cohesion

I have seen many areas in Lancashire and Yorkshire where second-, third-, and even fourth-generation Asians live in 'enclaves' of little Pakistan, Bangladesh, or India; no doubt there are many other similar areas in other parts of Britain. Their chances of integration are extremely limited; instead of making progress, some within these areas have, worryingly, regressed and totally disengaged from mainstream society.

The programme aims to:

- Enable young people to safely integrate into mainstream society
- Enable young people to understand British society and how they can play an integral part in it

Radicalisation / violent extremism

As mentioned earlier, there are some very confused and vulnerable young people. This programme would help them understand their role in society and help safeguard them from being radicalised, bringing some clarity into their lives.

The programmes aims to:

- Raise their understanding of violent extremism
- Enable them to recognise early signs of radicalisation

- Enable their understanding of how to raise issues and grievances effectively
- Provide a safe platform for young people to 'steam off'
- Provide a platform where they can hear perspectives on different cultures and faiths
- Enable them to broaden their horizons and strengthen their resolve

Mediation

Mediation would support those seeking to reconcile with their families. It would help young people rebuild relationships with their parents, help parents accept their children back into the family fold, and help both deal with any potential 'backlash'. This is an important final step in bringing families together.

I believe these initiatives would support those struggling to come to terms with the pressures of growing up without a sense of belonging, worth, or purpose and within conflicting cultures, perspectives, religious teachings, or differing norms. But more importantly, it would support those growing up with discrimination and lack of equal opportunity.

This paper was presented to an advisor at the Home Office through a very dear friend, Alan Mckie, without a response.

Chapter 25

On Reflection

Finding myself

On reflection, as ordinary as my life has been, from my childhood to the moment I retired as a police officer, I have had a lot to be grateful for.

That said, life has presented me with my fair share of trials and tribulations.

As a child in Pakistan, my survival was on a knife-edge. Far-off places and people could not be further from my mind—until my father came to England. Up to that point, I was content with running around, playing hide-and-seek, or dancing in the rain.

Despite moving to England, with free education and a liberal way of life, it did little to help me get my head out of the clouds. My fears of people, of making mistakes, but most of all, of my father all remained with me for several decades. All the possibilities and opportunities England offered failed to stop my fear of trying new things, to increase my desire to learn, and to stop me wishing my life away.

Before I met Marge, my one form of escapism was football; on the football pitch, I could truly be me. When my sons, Mehboob and Bashir, came along, they brought the kind of joy only children can. Yet even their joy failed to wake me, failed to help me find myself.

The truth is, I was always waiting for something or someone to come along and make things happen, never thinking I had to do it for myself.

My parents

My parents only ever wanted to do good. They were brought up to deal with life's hardship, the physical toil, and the lack of money. But to lose their only son to a way of life they had no comprehension of was a devastating blow. They had sacrificed so much, only to be kicked in the teeth when I walked out on my family.

Yet, they still found a way to always welcome me back to the family home with open arms. Finally seeing Marge with my mum was unforgettable and incredibly emotional. Marge had gone to visit my mum, at her request, on her deathbed, in hospital. It was the first and only time. Watching them communicate with each other was a site to behold. Neither could understand a word the other was saying, but the smile on their faces and the delight in their eyes clearly told them both what they mean to me. The sheer joy they had brought into my life in their own unique way became obvious to them at that precious moment.

I only ever realised my parents' true value when it was too late. I had not found the courage to share with them all the things I am grateful to them for. I see the sacrifices they made, what they taught me through their own unique struggles and ways, the words of wisdom they gave me, and their knowledge of the true meaning of living a life in the hope it may be of some benefit to others. They passed away without me being able to say any of the things I really wanted to say to them.

My sons

I destroyed their world when I walked out, yet they have found a way to forgive me my weaknesses. They love me unconditionally and continue to involve me in learning to piece together their shattered lives.

Mehboob, so happy and secure in his world as a child, was left to face his insecurities and grow up on his own. He has grown up to be a kind and caring man, yet his isolation has pushed him into the same world of my yesteryears.

Bashir, on the other hand, was so different, openly displaying his feelings and emotions. My leaving has had a profound effect on him too. Years of life without me has drained Bashir of his energy and zest for life. He, like his brother, has sunk into a place riddled with confusion and self-blame. Their glittering, happy eyes have been replaced with sad and sorrowful ones. At twenty-nine Bashir was diagnosed with bowel cancer, I believe this was partly due to the trauma he faced when I left. Yet with his grandfather's fighting spirit, he overcame this deadly disease.

I never realised the full extent of the damage I caused my sons when I walked out. I was too naive and wrapped up in my own selfish needs. Fortunately, I have awoken in time to realise what has happened, and we've begun to pull our lives together. I make no excuses for the pain I've caused them both. I simply developed far too late in life to have been able to stop it.

I am so proud of the kindness both Mehboob and Bashir have retained in a very uncertain and often unkind world.

Police culture

There are some aspects of the police culture I have already alluded to and touched upon earlier in the book. However, one aspect needs further reflection.

It's easy to forget that the police service started out as a male-only workforce. As women gradually joined, they were relegated to menial tasks. They were looked upon as if incapable of coping with the rigours of the macho police work and culture. As the service evolved and diversity within the workforce increased, those from different backgrounds, too, were made to struggle and were not readily accepted.

The culture, at various levels, allows some to surround themselves with those who look, think, and behave like them. They are unable or unwilling to accept those who are different—with some taking it upon themselves to make life difficult for those they see as outsiders. This is directed not only at those from different backgrounds but also at many white male officers who were not in their networks. They too became victims of an environment of bullying, harassment, and discrimination.

Those who found the courage to speak out were not believed, vilified, and labelled as troublemakers. Many suffered from ill health. Some were forced out and faced financial ruin. Others were forced to keep their heads down, as those in these cliques and networks closed ranks when someone dared to raise an issue or challenged them.

It's a culture that needs a radical change, with external intervention. In my view, the existing 'lessons learnt' process is not worth the paper it is written on. It amounts to nothing more than a slapped wrist. The make-up of the team reviewing any lessons learnt needs to be reconsidered. It should be made up of appropriate representatives from the local community, trade unions, relevant staff support networks, and HR. The HMIC should ask for evidence of how all forces have implemented any lessons learnt, what difference has been made and hold them to account for any failures.

Unfortunately, I have not seen any form of 'diversity' training or 'reforms' succeed in bringing about significant change to the police culture. Neither, unfortunately, have I seen enough will or determination by any government or the police service to genuinely tackle this issue.

Racism

It would be wrong of me to say that one form of discrimination is worse than another; they are all equally despicable and destructive.

However, due to my experience and role within the police service, I can only really comment on racism with some authority.

Words spoken, comments made, and actions taken due to our biases and prejudice, or our ignorance of difference have led to many shortened police careers; others left with incredible hurt and pain, simply because of their skin colour or their religious belief.

I have heard people say, time and again, that 'things have changed.' They claim, 'It's not how it used to be,' or say, 'The Macpherson report has dealt with racism.'

What my experience has shown me is that racism still exists. Pick up any newspaper, read any social media message; listen to any black footballer, athlete, actor, or those simply applying for jobs or seeking a service; and you will hear story upon story of racism. Yes, things have changed, but racism remains alive and kicking. Where previously it was overt, it is now more subtle. Modern forms of social media make it easier for racists to hide behind anonymity. Racism, like other forms of discrimination, will only be 'done' once a person's background becomes irrelevant.

During my years of experience with the police service, I can categorically say that, for every successful employment tribunal on the grounds of racism, there would be at least a hundred that never got to that stage. Many were buried almost as soon as they were raised, as they were either discredited or the closing of ranks made it impossible to proceed.

Throughout my ten years as chair of the LBPA, every single BAME member of staff who had a cause to speak to me stated he or she had suffered some form of racism, ranging from pathetic attempts at humour to fabrications of evidence. Only a handful had the confidence to report it.

Damage caused by some BAME staff

In my view, there is only one thing worse than the behaviour of racists, and that is the behaviour of a small number of BAME police officers and staff themselves.

Those among this small group have perhaps allowed themselves to be institutionalised to the point where they lack tolerance for their BAME colleagues and communities and resent their own kind. The behaviour of some of them has demonstrated how desperate they have been to fit in with their white colleagues and to prove that they're different to others from their background. Some have been lured by false promises of promotion or lateral progression, which leads them to abandon their roots and forget who they are. They pick on and ridicule their BAME colleagues and overzealously police their own communities, just to impress their white colleagues or those they think will help their careers. Their behaviour, in some cases, does result in short-lived success. But ultimately, it leaves them broken and demoralised. They learn the hard way who they really are.

Sadly, very few of those who went down this road realised the damage they caused to their BAME colleagues and communities and, ultimately, to themselves.

Some, because of guilt or shame, further alienate themselves, avoiding contact with those of their own kind and find seeking help very difficult, coping as best they can on their own. Those who do seek help and are able to share their experiences, often due to the skills of the person dealing with them, gradually begin to accept support. The support, provided sensitively and over a long period of time, eventually helps them come to terms with what they've gone through, understand their behaviour, deal with their shattered egos and ambitions, and rebuild their careers and relationships with their BAME colleagues.

For them to seek such help and support takes immense courage. The response from those offering support needs to be equally courageous and understanding.

Effecting change

Looking back on my time with Lancashire Constabulary, I didn't know it then, but I now realise it was all about bringing about change, however small—change for the public I served; my colleagues; Lancashire Constabulary; and, most significantly, myself.

Bringing about change for the public was limited. They were the victims of others' behaviour. There was little I could do to prevent them from becoming victims. But whenever I was called upon to deal with them, I made sure my response was sensitive, empathetic, and showed genuine desire to listen and help.

I was able to bring about some change for my colleagues, in two distinctly different ways. For my BAME colleagues, it was by supporting them when they needed someone to turn to, by raising their issues and concerns, by challenging policies and practices, and by providing them with a collective voice. For my white colleagues, it was by facilitating workshops and discussions on difference and helping to raise their awareness and understanding. Sadly, this took place far too late in my career and reached too small a number to have made a significant difference. But it did bring about some change, however small, in their thinking and behaviour.

Bringing about change within Lancashire Constabulary was perhaps the most difficult. This was not something a mere PC could do alone. However, for some senior officers—through meetings, two-way mentoring processes, providing alternative solutions to difficult policing issues, and simply acting as a conduit between them and minority communities, I was able to bring about some change.

Compared with what was required, what I did, admittedly, was a drop in the ocean. It needed a much more joined-up approach and not to be done in isolation. To have brought about the desired change, it needed a collective approach by the Home Secretary and the police service, supported by the NBPA and the local BPAs.

In all honesty, I got to a position of some influence far too late in my career and too close to my retirement to have begun the process of bringing all the local and national staff support networks and associations together to address difference collectively. I was able to achieve this at the local level, representing the other staff associations and networks at the constabulary's strategic forums.

I will always be thankful for the opportunities that came my way, enabling me to do what little I could.

Learning from others

Life, they say, is a mystery. To some extent I should know; it has taken me nearly forty years to fathom out some of its basics.

However, as I now reflect on some aspects of my life, I know I've learnt from many people. I learnt the desire to help others from my parents. Marge taught me about love and devotion. I learnt kindness and forgiveness from my two sons.

I've been fortunate to have had the opportunity to get some understanding of people different to me by moving to a country where those from a variety of backgrounds and cultures live side by side. I learnt from my early experiences—being attacked by boys in Oxford and Bradford, my friendships with Shantilal and Mark, and my first fight at a school in Bradford. And finally, I've learnt from the many people I've worked, played, and socialised with. Some I have already mentioned.

Others I will always be indebted to include:

- *Tariq Javed.* It would be very remiss of me not to start with the first Asian officer to work for Lancashire Constabulary. Tariq found his professional life a challenge. He endured the worst aspects of betrayal and discrimination I have ever come across. There is no one who has shared with me more of their personal pains, trials, and tribulations related to being a minority police officer. His courage to share what he went through helped me understand the level of racism within the police service.

However, Tariq was born to be a police officer—someone who would always put the needs of the public first. It is such a shame that someone dedicated to making things better for others was made to suffer, rather than be allowed to do what he'd always dreamt of doing. His determination and desire to come through it all with dignity has amazed and inspired me. His experiences and suffering provided me with invaluable insight to my role as the chair of the Lancashire Black Police Association. I still feel his pain, as I think about some of the experiences, he shared with me.

- *Andy Pratt.* Andy retired as a superintendent from the constabulary a few years before me, but his desire and commitment to helping others has never left him. He continues to find new ways to support and guide people of all faiths and from all backgrounds, whether it's through politics, his charitable work, or his religious beliefs. Mention his name among different communities across Lancashire, and straight away, people will step forward with a brimming smile and a story to share of his help, support, and guidance.

  Andy continues to share his knowledge and his much sought-after wisdom whenever I call upon him.

- *Tunde Zack Williams.* Tundi was a lecturer at the University of Central Lancashire when we first me. He kindly agreed to provide me a greater understanding of equality and diversity. Tundi became my mentor, opening a wealth of knowledge for me to eagerly absorb. We began to meet at the NBPA conferences and charity dinners, becoming close friends. Tundi is a true gentleman, and I was incredibly fortunate to have met him. I am privileged to have him as a friend.

- *Lukmaan Mulla.* Lukmaan is one of the most intellectually gifted and articulate police officers I have ever come across. He never joined the LBPA for reasons of his own, and I respected him for that. He had a voice and strength of character that allowed him to articulate his thoughts, which he put to good use by helping others. He never failed to provide support for anyone who went to him.

   Lukmaan was always there for me, from the very first moment he walked into my office, sharing his thoughts on many areas of policing, and helping me with much-needed alternative perspectives. His unique and subtle way of challenging my thought processes helped me broaden my understanding of the police service and many of the people working within it.

- *Justin Srivastava.* Justin was the first BAME officer to be promoted to the rank of chief inspector in Lancashire and currently serves as a superintendent. He was also my vice chair, providing me with a much-needed strategic perspective of the police service. He never tired of my typical 'PC plod' questions and was so generous with his time. Coming from a mixed-race background, Justin was able to raise my awareness of the unique challenges faced by those from such backgrounds, which he did with patience, tact, and diplomacy.

He remains a much valued and trusted friend.

- *Judith Finney.* Judith was an inspector within the community safety and partnerships department at our HQ. Her advice and support was immensely valuable for the LBPA. Judith went out of her way to support the work of the LBPA and other staff support networks. She readily made herself available whenever I needed someone to talk to. Through our work together, we became and remain good friends.

- *Noel Coombes.* Noel was the only black journalist I ever knew, but he was a journalist with a soul and a conscious. During our brief relationship, he introduced me to the African Caribbean communities in Preston and some of the work he was involved in to bring these communities together.

  Unfortunately, Noel passed away shortly after we met. He was a well-known and much respected man, who will be sorely missed by all those who knew him.

- *John Walkley.* I was introduced to John by Thelma before she left to work for the RBS group. John is very articulate, incredibly knowledgeable, and has a wicked sense of humour. He runs his own business—working with senior professionals from many sectors in their professional growth and development. Through his friendship, he has brought much-needed professionalism to many areas of my work. It was John who first taught me to understand the benefits of discretionary time and helped me put time management at the centre of my thought processes.

  He is a much-valued friend, who constantly challenges my thinking in his own unique way, helping me to expand my comfort zones.

- Then there is *Ann-Marie Bull*. Ann-Marie, I wish you had given me that material from your dream. It would have brought much needed excitement to this book. I still smile about that moment you shared your dream with me.

There were also others, whose details I am unable to share, who all played an important part in my learning and in shaping the person I am today.

My Alice

It took years of deep devotion, tons of patience, and an astronomical amount of love from a woman who, until we met, existed only in the deepest recesses of my mind—a woman who helped to put me on the road to self-discovery.

I often think my shy and introverted personality, a kind of illness, could never be cured through medicinal recourse but only by the love of a woman I was destined to meet. It has been my good fortune to have met Marge or 'my Alice', as I affectionately call her by her middle name. She continues to challenge, thrill, and excite me, all in one breath. I know I can never fully repay my debt to her. When we first met, I wish I had some of the ability; knowledge; experience; and, most important of all, confidence I now have. It may have helped Marge when she was going through much anguish and suffering, trying to support me.

She has a twinkle in her eyes that still shines bright, and my love for her continues to grow. We have a deep-rooted connection that, despite our challenges and different cultures and backgrounds, keeps us very much together.

Meeting and being with Marge was my kismet, my destiny.

Mahmood Ahmed

Leaving my little village behind in Pakistan, the move to Yorkshire, the closing of textile mills in Bradford, the move to Blackburn, the closing of the Darwen depot, and the change of my bus route—these were all the paths that led to our meeting.

It had to be my kismet. What else could it be?

***

In concluding my life's journey thus far, I would say that, for many years, I struggled to understand my surroundings and environment and their impact on me. As a young boy in Pakistan, I was fortunate to survive illnesses that took my elder siblings. For some reason, listening to my grandmother telling me stories about my father inadvertently created more fear than admiration. This was something I was unable to deal with until late into my thirties, and even then, I never managed to talk to my father about it. The move to England provided opportunities to grow and develop in ways not possible in Pakistan, yet the fear of failing and making mistakes crippled my growth and development— taking away any desire to try something new.

This—what can I call it? —inner turmoil of my self-created prison continued even after I became an adult, after I got married and had children. I was unable to pull myself out of the deep dark hole I had put myself in. I failed at school and ended up doing a mundane job. Yet even in the deepest part of my head or the highest cloud I floated on, I remembered some words of wisdom from my father and the learnings from early experiences, which helped develop a desire to do good, to help others, and to try and make a difference.

Then came along a very special lady, along with my father's words, helping me to slowly awaken, to understand my past and my experiences, and to at long last find a sense of purpose. The transformation I've gone through has helped me understand others and better understand myself, come to terms with my past, and look to the future with optimism—not fear or anxiety.

Whatever my failings were and are, they are all due to me. However, whatever limited ability I have developed to see things from others' perspective is due to all the wonderful people who have enriched my life, none more so than the lady always beside me.

I thank the almighty and everyone for their role in helping me to find myself.

Printed and bound by CPI Group (UK) Ltd, Croydon, CR0 4YY